Money can be confusing and even overw[...] [barcode: T0311134] [...]e
Ben cuts through the noise with simple, [...] [...]v
to do better. Jargon free and straight to the point, this book is a must-read
for anyone serious about unlocking their inner millionaire.

— **Victoria Devine**, founder and author of *She's on the Money*

Getting wealthy doesn't just happen by accident. Like being successful
in any endeavour, it takes time, focus, and an intelligent approach. It also
comes down to doing the right things at the right time as you progress
through life's key milestones. If you want to get (or be) wealthy, trying to
figure it all out on your own can be overwhelming, however, Ben Nash
makes it easier with practical tips and his easy-to-understand approach.
This reduces the anxiety when making some of your investment decisions,
or at the very least, empowers you to ask the right questions. Ben's focus
on the different financial stages and how to move through them faster and
easier allows readers to make more progress, avoid common pitfalls, and do
it all without making drastic lifestyle sacrifices.

— **Grant Hackett**, CEO of Genlife and Olympic Gold Medal Athlete

If you want honest advice and a step-by-step guide on how to get rich, then
you're going to love this book! Should you invest in property or shares?
What are the secret financial strategies of the rich? And more importantly,
how can you use this information to get ahead in your own life? Ben answers
all these questions and more. You're going to love this!

— **Queenie Tan**, founder of @investwithqueenie

Ben has once again nailed it! With clear, actionable steps and invaluable
insights, this is the ultimate guide on wealth-building for millennials to
reach their first million and beyond. A must-read for anyone ready to take
control of their financial future.

— **Fred Schebesta**, founder of Finder.com.au

I've applied several strategies discussed in *Virgin Millionaire* and I'm already
over halfway to becoming a millionaire at 26. Ben's insights on leverage, tax
considerations, and how property and shares work together to build wealth

are particularly valuable. This book is an excellent and practical guide to becoming a millionaire.

— **Natasha Etschmann AKA Tash Invests,**
co-author of *How to Not Work Forever*

Making your first million is hard. But *Virgin Millionaire* makes it easier. In this book, Ben outlines the simple steps to build a solid financial foundation in order to get ahead quicker. Setting up your ideal future doesn't have to come at the expense of your life now. Instead, Ben outlines that you can set yourself up financially *and* enjoy your journey there.

— **Ana Kresina,** co-author of *How to Not Work Forever* and
author of *Kid's Ain't Cheap*

Read it. Apply it. Make money from it. *Virgin Millionaire* is the practical guidebook for everyone who wants to learn the skills to master your money, forever. If you're serious about your money, I encourage you to read this book and follow Ben's action items and implement them as soon as you can!

— **Jessica Brady,** Money Expert

If you want to get seriously wealthy, this book is an absolute must read! Ben breaks down the key stages of money from just getting started all the way to being a multimillionaire — and it's all backed up with exactly what you need to do to make progress to each stage faster. For readers, Ben's practical approach and explanation of the specific frameworks and tactics you can use to get more out of the money you have today, and set up your ideal future while you enjoy today is a game changer for anyone that is serious about their money and getting ahead.

— **Robbo Roper,** founder of Trusted Finance and Australia's
most followed mortgage expert

For those earning good income and confused as to how to make the most of it, this book is a game-changer. Ben has built a career helping people focus on the most important things across each stage of wealth accumulation, starting with a self-assessment of where they are 'at financially', and identifying the most crucial steps forward.

— **Clayton Daniel,** CEO of Ensombl, the leading digital
platform for financial advice professionals

VIRGIN MILLIONAIRE

MILLIONAIRE

THE STEP-BY-STEP GUIDE TO YOUR FIRST MILLION AND BEYOND

BEN NASH

WILEY

First published in 2024 by John Wiley & Sons Australia, Ltd
Level 4, 600 Bourke St, Melbourne, Victoria 3000, Australia

Typeset in Adobe Caslon Pro 11/15pt

© John Wiley & Sons Australia, Ltd 2024

The moral rights of the author have been asserted

ISBN: 978-1-394-25591-7

A catalogue record for this
book is available from the
NATIONAL
LIBRARY National Library of Australia
OF AUSTRALIA

Cover design by Alex Ross Creative

Printed and bound by CPI Group (UK) Ltd, Croydon, CR0 4YY

C9781394255917_021024

Disclaimer
The material in this publication is of the nature of general comment only,
and does not represent professional advice. It is not intended to provide
specific guidance for particular circumstances and it should not be relied
on as the basis for any decision to take action or not take action on any
matter which it covers. Readers should obtain professional advice where
appropriate, before making any such decision. To the maximum extent
permitted by law, the author and publisher disclaim all responsibility and
liability to any person, arising directly or indirectly from any person taking
or not taking action based on the information in this publication.

Contents

About the author

If you're not familiar with me or Pivot Wealth, you might be wondering why I'm the best person to help you become a Virgin Millionaire.

I'm a financial adviser and the founder of Pivot Wealth, Australia's most awarded money management company that helps people invest smarter to create a life not limited by money (or a lack of it). I'm deeply passionate about helping people make better money choices so they can live better lives. Through my work I draw on my practical experience to simplify the often-overwhelming field of investing and wealth creation by distilling complex tactics into simple, practical, actionable steps.

I'm Australia's most followed financial adviser on social media and am a speaker, podcaster and financial educator. I write regularly for news.com.au, and I'm the author of *Get Unstuck* (2018) and *Replace Your Salary by Investing* (2023).

My content is authentic, practical, to the point and jargon-free. It's designed to drive rapid implementation and rapid results.

Unlike most financial advisers in Australia I've chosen to focus on people in their thirties and forties who are still building their investments and wealth to achieve financial independence. And unlike traditional financial advice, my work has a strong focus on lifestyle alongside money outcomes, something I feel is crucial to driving a money plan that will actually work for you.

I'm a finance geek at heart. I have two Master's degrees in finance, together with a number of professional financial-advice qualifications. That said, the concepts in this book are drawn mainly from my practical experience.

For seven consecutive years I have been formally listed among the Financial Standard Top 50 Most Influential Financial Advisers in Australia. I have been named the Independent Financial Adviser (IFA) Industry Thought Leader of the Year, Innovator of the Year (twice), Practice Principal of the Year, Best Social Network, Association of Financial Advisers Excellence in Education Award, and Best Client Servicing Financial Adviser in Australia. Pivot Wealth has been recognised as Australia's Best Client Servicing Financial Advice Firm, and Marketing Program of the Year (twice), and as a finalist for Wellness Program of the Year, Digital Advice Strategy of the Year, Women's Community Program of the Year, Self Licensed Firm of the Year and SME Employer of the Year. Pivot has also been listed among the *Australian Financial Review*'s 100 Fastest Growing Companies in Australia, *AFR*'s Most Innovative Companies and *AFR Boss* Best Places to Work.

I've partnered with leading organisations to deliver financial education content, including working with the National Rugby League (NRL) to create and deliver their financial education program for all professional male and female NRL players. We've also delivered content for the Australian Government, Newscorp, GlaxoSmithKline, WeWork, Pearler, SelfWealth, Raiz Invest, Volt Bank, Work-Shop and Publicis Media, among others.

In addition to my work at Pivot, I'm a co-founder of Ensombl, Australia's biggest community of Financial Advisers. Ensombl is dedicated to driving the positive evolution of Financial Advice in Australia and around the world.

Having advised and coached over a thousand people directly through one-on-one financial advice, and educated millions more through my content, I've found what really works (and what doesn't).

Understanding what's really possible gives you the confidence to make the smartest money choices. I believe passionately that every person should be able to experience the sense of empowerment, and relief, that comes from knowing your money is sorted. I feel very privileged to be able to help people make this happen for them.

Virgin Millionaire

(noun phrase)

Someone who has built or is building $1 million or more in wealth without the advantage of a trust fund, windfall or a big leg-up from their family.

Introduction

Getting rich is easy.

You need to spend less than you earn, and invest the difference.

I could sign off there, but if it were that easy we'd all be rich already. Over the past couple of decades I've spent a *lot* of time thinking about money and how to get more of it without drastic lifestyle sacrifices. What I've learned is that the secret to real money success lies more in what holds people *back* than in what drives them *forward*.

While everyone's situation is unique, there are some common challenges that stop people from being financially successful.

The first is the information overload that is the result of too many options and too much information. If you've ever done any research into money or investing, you'll know that it's easy to be overwhelmed. It's like drinking from a fire hose. That there are so many mixed messages, conflicting opinions and hidden agendas makes it even harder. It's hard to know who to listen to, let alone who to trust.

The second big challenge is that people struggle to find the right balance between living well today and planning for the future. You want to make progress, but you also have needs today, and striking the right balance is hard.

The third barrier, which is potentially the biggest, is the fear of making a mistake. Any time you're considering making a new investment, implementing a new strategy or changing your approach, the fear of missing something that will come back to bite you is real. You don't want to do something dumb that you'll regret later, and that fear can be paralysing.

This can leave you stuck, repeating what you've been doing. You risk missing the opportunity to get more out of what you have today in order to get better results faster.

Through this book I'm going to help you overcome these challenges and position yourself to take confident action. This is crucial to your success in the short and the long term, as it's the one thing that will start building your money momentum and this, in turn, will make your next steps easier.

Your cash is going backwards

Most people don't realise it, but if you have your money in cash, it's going backwards.

This is true whether your money is in physical cash or an everyday bank account, or it's sitting in a high-interest savings account.

You might think I'm crazy for saying this, because when you look in your bank account the balance is probably increasing, or at least staying at the same level. But if you're looking at the balance alone, what you don't see is the real impact of taxes and inflation.

Interest income is taxable (I'll get into this in more detail later), and under the current tax rates and rules, if you earn above $45k per annum, your marginal tax rate plus Medicare levy is at least 32 per cent, meaning you lose at least a third of your interest income in tax.

You can calculate your after-tax interest rate by using the following formula. We've used the current highest interest rate savings account, which was 5.55 per cent in March 2024.

$$\text{After-tax interest rate} = (1 - \text{marginal tax rate}) \times \text{before-tax interest rate}$$

In this case:

$$\text{After-tax interest rate} = (1 - 32\%) \times 5.55\%$$
$$= 3.77\%$$

But then you need to account for inflation.

With inflation, the cost of goods and services are increasing every year. Over the 12 months to December 2023, the rate of inflation was 4.1 per cent, meaning that on average costs increased by just over 4 per cent.

When looking at the 'real' return on any investment, you need to look at your after-tax return, then take away inflation:

$$\text{Real return} = \text{after-tax return} - \text{inflation}$$

Plugging in the number from our previous example:

$$\text{Real return} = \text{after-tax return (3.77\%)} - \text{inflation (4.1\%)}$$
$$= -0.33\%$$

This shows that in 'real' (after inflation and tax) terms, any money you have in savings today will be worth less in a year's time. Your savings balance may have increased but your money has actually gone backwards, so you're further behind. Over the long term, this is a total disaster that should be avoided at all costs.

So what can you do instead?

If you want your money to grow, you need to use investments with higher long-term returns. Table I.1 (overleaf) includes data from Vanguard and Canstar showing the 30-year long-term returns on various investments.

You can see from this table that all investments outside of cash and bonds have much higher long-term investment returns, so if you want your money actually to grow after taxes and inflation, you need to be investing.

Table I.1 30-year returns on different investments

Investment type	Annual returns (%)
Australian shares	9.8
US shares	11.7
International shares	9.1
Australian-listed property	9.3
Australian bonds	6
Cash	4.4

Source: Vanguard Australia and Canstar.

The power of compounding

Time and money combined is a powerful thing. Consider this example:

Starting with $0 today, you save and invest $10 each day. Assuming the long-term return on Australian shares of 9.8 per cent, over 20 years this $10 a day will grow to $225 072. Over 20 years you will have saved a total of $73 000, with the rest of the work being done by compound interest, which delivers a total growth return of $152 072 on top of the money you've saved and invested.

In my opinion this is a pretty good result for the cost of a couple of cups of coffee a day. But it gets even better.

If you keep investing $10 daily for another ten years, your money will grow to $658 912. During this 10-year period you will have invested another $36 500, with compound interest adding an extra $397 340.

Keep going, and after another 10 years (40 years total) your investments will grow to $1 810 267. You invest the same $36 500 over this period, but compound interest delivers you over a million dollars ($1 114 855).

To hammer home this point, give it another 10 years and your money will grow to $4 865 816. With the same $36 500 invested, compounding over these 10 years will add $3 019 049 to your investment bottom line.

Saving and investing $10 a day isn't nothing, particularly in the current cost-of-living crisis. I get that a lot of people would find this challenging, but is it doable? I think the answer is yes. And further, there should be points throughout your life when you could invest a whole lot more than $10 a day.

As I said at the start of this chapter, success is simple. But if it's this easy, why doesn't everyone do it?

To start investing you need confidence, and to keep going you need motivation. The confidence to get started is crucial, because most people get stuck at the starting line, often for years (sometimes decades). The power of motivation is hugely underestimated when it comes to money, but how motivated you are to keep pushing forward is the single biggest results driver, once you get things moving.

Creating confidence

The fact you're reading this book tells me you know that doing something is important, and hopefully the $10-a-day example has helped to solidify this thinking. But knowing you need to do something isn't enough. If you want to get results and outcomes you will need to act. And confidence will be crucial.

Most people get stuck at the starting line, or at least take less action than what's needed, because they lack the confidence that comes from knowing the action they're about to take is the right one for them.

When you know that the action you're about to take is the best one and that it can't go wrong, you're going to crank it. As a result, you'll take maximum action and drive maximum results sooner.

In his book *The Catalyst* (2022), Jonah Berger talks through the huge amount of research that has proved that humans have an innate tendency to avoid uncertainty, even if it means paying a significant price.

One example he shares is an experiment in which people were offered the choice between being given a guaranteed $30, or having an 80 per cent chance of receiving $45. Most people chose the guaranteed $30, even though the expected payoff of the gamble was higher.

If you were to run this game 10 times, with the guaranteed $30 you'd receive 10 × $30 = $300, and the second option with an 80 per cent probability would give you 8 × $45 = $360. The first option is guaranteed to make you 20 per cent less, but it's the choice most people pick because it delivers a more certain outcome.

When it comes to money, there is uncertainty any time you make a change. As a Virgin Millionaire, you'll be making changes from a position of inexperience, which means the uncertainty levels will be even higher.

This uncertainty can be managed and reduced by leveraging the tools I'm going to cover in the chapters that follow. But if becoming wealthy is important to you, you should accept now that there will be times when things will get a little uncomfortable. This is a completely natural part of the journey.

When you know uncertainty is looming, you can prepare yourself to navigate effectively through it. Some of the tools and tactics you'll discover as you work through this book will help set you up for success. But the short version is that knowledge is power and building your understanding of money, investing and how to plan will go a long way to giving you complete confidence that the move you need to make next to unlock the next level of results is the very best one for you.

I want this book to be the catalyst that drives your knowledge and positions you to smash your next steps with total confidence.

Driving motivation

To state the obvious, as a financial planner I help people set up financial plans. When we put these plans together, it often takes robust, and sometimes challenging, conversations to help people decide on their path forward. But ultimately the path people choose to follow leads to good financial outcomes.

But not everyone achieves the results they plan for. When this happens, I take it a little bit personally. I want my clients to succeed. I want to see them hit their lifestyle targets, and I want them to create true money success. Falling short is a big disappointment, for them and for me.

There can be a lot of reasons why a plan doesn't work out. But ultimately, in almost every case, it boils down to the client not taking the action needed. It's easy (and natural) to explain away this lack of action — something unexpected happened, the targets weren't quite right, or there just was 'too much going on' to focus on money.

Ultimately, though, the real reason is that the client wasn't motivated enough. Not that they weren't motivated. It was just that their motivation levels weren't quite high enough to drive the necessary action.

I've spent a lot of time thinking about barriers to motivation, and through this thinking, and a lot of conversations with my clients, I believe I've found the single biggest roadblock.

In the early stages of growing your money, the progress is slowest. I can tell you for sure that no matter where you are today, the progress you'll make in the next ten years will be the slowest it will ever be.

Going back to our example of investing $10 a day, I showed how in the final 10 years your investment growth would be more than $3 million. This is pure growth on top of $36 500 of savings you put in *and* in addition to the money you already have in your investment account. This is clearly pretty awesome and would make for a pretty exciting 10 years.

Wind back to the first 10 years, when your investments grew by a relatively modest $25 098. You put in the same $36 500 in this 10-year period, but because you hadn't *yet* built your money momentum, the investment growth was small compared to how much you put in.

But here's the thing. The effort you put in through those first 10 years is the only thing that delivers the $3 million of growth in the last 10. Without the work done in these first 10 years, the results in the last 10 won't be possible.

The real risk, and the trap most people fall into, is thinking that because the growth and progress in the first 10 years aren't very substantial, it's okay to do less, or nothing at all. So they aim to save and invest more and make more progress at some undefined later point in time, when this seems like it will be easier.

But money doesn't work this way.

Regardless of where you want to get to, you have to put in the early work. You can choose to do this early work in your twenties, or you can choose to do it in your fifties. But the later you get started, the more work you will have to do to reach the same position or level of wealth. And the longer you leave it, the more likely it is you'll be forced to settle for an outcome significantly below what you really want.

If this is you, the good news is that you've come to the right place. Through this book I'm going to help you build the confidence to take your next step, whether it's to start investing, or investing more, or investing smarter with tax. This will help you drive more growth and progress into the future.

I'm also going to help you build your motivation muscle so you will create a repeatable process that will keep your motivation levels high for the years to come. This will help you keep following the Virgin Millionaire pathway to some pretty epic results.

I'm not saying it will be easy, but I will give you all the tools you need to make it happen. And I can tell you, the results will be worth it.

Stages of money

There will always be a lot of things you *could* do with your money, but there's only so many things you *can* do at any one point in time. And while taking action is important, not all actions will have the same impact. Some things will move the dial more than others.

The most important and valuable actions for you will depend on where you're at with your money. For example, taking on debt to invest might be a great idea for someone who has consistent savings and a full emergency fund, but a total disaster for someone just getting started. Making tax-deductible super contributions could be really smart for someone in their forties who has a couple of properties and a nice share portfolio; for someone in their twenties it could mean a costly delay in buying their first property.

When people talk about money and their investment options, most speak in absolute terms: shares are good; property is good, debt is bad; super is good/bad/ugly. But in reality they can all be good or bad. It depends on you and the stage you're at.

Over the past decade I've often applied the 'stages of money' framework when advising clients, and in that time I feel I've cracked the code that enables you to figure out which moves make sense and which would be a mistake. This framework may not be common knowledge, but it is the key to true success and making the maximum financial progress in the minimum time.

To be clear, I'm not talking about making fast money. There's plenty of evidence that quick-fix solutions don't work. What I'm talking about is achieving the results you want in a sustainable way, so your progress is reliable and consistent through the years ahead. This will help you get your money moving forward in the shortest time possible with what you have to work with today.

Through *Virgin Millionaire*, I'm going to take you behind the curtain and unpack the lessons I've learned while helping people build, collectively, *over a billion dollars* in investments and wealth, so you can use this knowledge to accelerate your own progress.

I've codified the five key stages people go through with their money, what defines the stages themselves and, importantly, what you can do to complete each stage and take it to the next level. I call these the Smart Money Stages. They create the platform that should direct your financial focus at every single step from here until you achieve what I refer to as *smart money freedom*.

Smart money freedom means the amount of money you have in investments will allow you to live your ideal lifestyle. You can do all the things you want to do: travel when and how you want; provide for your family and loved ones, and support any causes that are important to you; live where you want; spend on whatever you value most, and never have to worry about whether you have enough money.

I call this final Smart Money Stage the Impact stage, because your money is fully sorted, you can direct your personal focus to having the impact you want on the world and the people around you.

Sorry to be a party pooper, but achieving this is going to take some time, a bit of work and a lot of focus. Everyone starts somewhere, and no matter where you are right now, you're exactly where you need to be.

I'll start by helping you set up rock-solid financial Foundations. From there, we'll advance through the next three stages, Focus, Optimise and Accelerate, to arrive at the Impact stage. Through each stage, I'll help you understand *exactly* what you need to do next, where you should focus and the things that will best move the dial of your progress.

I want to call out early that I believe that money success is a journey and not just a destination. Unlike the wildly popular FI/RE (financial independence, retire early) movement, which requires that you make drastic sacrifices today to become financially free sooner, I want you to enjoy yourself while you're working towards your version of money success. This is an important part of what will make this approach effective and sustainable for you into the years ahead.

Aiming for bigger goals

I've worked with many people over the years who have had plenty of support to help them with their money. It might have come from family, friends or colleagues they like and trust. But often my clients have bigger goals than those achieved by the people around them.

For past generations things were a little simpler. Most people had two big financial goals: to buy and pay off a home, and to squirrel away enough money to retire by 65. If you were ambitious, you might throw in being able to afford an annual holiday down on the South Coast at Christmas time.

Most young people today want a lot more. The dream home in a nice area without a hectic commute. The ability to travel overseas regularly without pinching pennies. Enough money to work because you want to rather than because you have to, and to do this well before you reach 65. And flexibility in the way you can enjoy your lifestyle and spend time with your family and loved ones.

These are all epic things I think everyone can (and borderline should) have, and they're things that are absolutely possible to achieve. But they're also *seriously expensive*. To put this into context, at the time of writing, the average cost of a property in Australia is $753654, and the average income is $98218.

I explain these calculations in chapter 1, but the short version for now is that you'll need around $2 million in investments to deliver you an annual income at the Australian average.

This means that the average cost of financial freedom today is almost $3 million. This comes from $2 million in investments to generate your income, plus almost $1 million for the cost of owning an average home, mortgage free.

To put it another way, if you have $3 million in cash today, you can afford to buy an average property and invest what's left over to pay you the Australian average income each year for the rest of your life. And every year you don't have that much money, your goal gets bigger and further away, because the cost of property is going up and the average income is also increasing.

That $3 million is a significant sum of money, and something that will take most people a serious amount of time and focus to build. And the big thing to call out here is that most people I talk to don't want to live an average life. Average is unlikely to deliver your dream home, the ability to spend the way you really want to, and to live your real ideal lifestyle.

So that means that your real target is probably a fair bit higher. Don't get too caught up on the numbers now, because in chapter 1 I'm going to show you how you can calculate exactly how much money you will need to achieve your version of financial freedom.

Not to spoil the surprise, but the end result is that you're going to be a multimillionaire. What's more, you will probably be in a position that exceeds that of previous generations in your family and other people in your circle. Maybe I should have called this book 'Virgin Multimillionaire', but I hope you get the point.

Virgin Millionaires are nailing it with their money to get to a position that exceeds that enjoyed by the people they know and love. They do this not out of some sense of competitiveness or even because they want to be really rich, but simply because this is the amount of money they need to live the lifestyle they choose.

Yes, there is some serious work to be done here, but the good news is that people today, and young people in particular, have a few advantages that put them in a strong position.

They have time on their side, and the power of time over money is a beautiful thing. They also have much higher incomes today than at any time in history, which creates a big opportunity for saving and investing. But perhaps the biggest advantage is that young people now actually recognise how important it is to get good at money and investing.

This understanding is the first step, which helps drive the confidence to get started. Then it will help create motivation. From there it's simply a matter of applying the right tactics at the right times to keep your money moving forward.

This is what I'm going to help you do through this book. Now let me be the first to officially welcome you to your future.

Happy reading.

Ben

CHAPTER 1

The Smart Money Stages

Paul and Lara were a couple in their early forties with two young kids. Paul worked as an executive making a really strong salary, and Lara worked in marketing and was just getting back into the work groove after five years of maternity leave followed by part-time work.

They had some really good things going on with their money, but when we started working together, I discovered they'd made some serious mistakes that were holding them back. We realised that if these issues weren't fixed, and quickly, they'd essentially be stuck with working forever.

Paul and Lara had bought their own home a while back and made some good money as it increased in value. Their savings capacity was strong so they purchased a lovely lifestyle property on the NSW South Coast, a place they could enjoy with their family.

Paul had set up a trust for investing based on some research he'd done and advice from friends in a similar position. He had started doing some ETF investing through this trust to generate another income stream for their future.

Things were going along pretty well, and Paul and Lara were happy, but then everything changed…

Through the 2023 interest-rate-tightening cycle, the repayments on the debt on Paul and Lara's home and their lifestyle property started crimping their cashflow. They weren't struggling, but they weren't able to save very much at all. They were treading water financially.

When we started getting into the detail, we realised there were a few issues at play. First, while their home had made them money through its growth, they had a large mortgage on this property. When interest rates were ultra-low, around 2 per cent, this was fine, but in a normal interest-rate environment it meant a huge chunk of their income was needed to cover their repayments.

Further, the lifestyle property they had was awesome, but having around a million dollars in debt to service on a property that wasn't generating any income was a challenge. It meant a cashflow cost for the repayments themselves, but it also meant Paul and Lara couldn't borrow more money to make further property investments.

And while I love trusts as an investment structure (I will dive into these later), because there wasn't a lot of money invested through this investment account, it was costing more for the annual tax returns than the amount of tax that was being saved—by a significant margin.

You'd be forgiven for thinking that Paul and Lara were doing all the smart things with their money. Buy a home, smart. Set up a trust, smart. Buy ETFs, smart. Buy a lifestyle property, lovely.

The real issue here isn't that these moves weren't good things to do; it was that the timing was wrong relative to the other things that were going on with their money. As a result, their progress suffered.

And that's the thing with money, you have to not only do good things; you have to do them at a good time.

Unpacking the Smart Money Stages

This is a concept I'll refer to throughout this book, so it's worth unpacking here.

From my experience with helping people with their money directly through one-on-one advice, and indirectly through my education content, I've found there are five key stages people go through on their money journey (figure 1.1). The good news is that if you know what to look for and what to do at each of these stages, you can accelerate your progress and put yourself in the best possible position sooner.

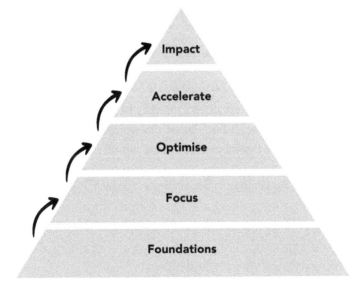

Figure 1.1 the five Smart Money Stages

There are a lot of different labels given to true money success: financial freedom, financial independence, financial security, financial stability, abundance, independence, and the list goes on. I refer to this as 'smart money freedom' and my definition is simple. *You own your home, mortgage free, and have sufficient investments to provide enough income to live your ideal lifestyle.*

For a Virgin Millionaire, smart money freedom is something you need to achieve without a trust fund or massive leg-up from family. It's something that will take years, often decades to achieve. But the juice really is worth the squeeze.

Fast forward into the future. You've achieved smart money freedom. You now have enough money rolling into your bank account every week or month to allow you to live your ideal lifestyle without ever having to work again.

This isn't to say you won't work. Most people I talk to about this don't actually want to retire. They're often hardworking high achievers who have deep passions and a solid skill set, and they want to be and feel productive.

But there's a huge difference between working because you need the money and working because you choose to. The feeling of having a choice is a total game changer.

Smart money freedom is exactly what I'm going to help you to plan and prepare for and, ultimately, to create as you work through this book. We're going to do this knowing you can make it happen on your own without a huge leg-up from your family. And we're going to assume you don't have other people in your family or close circle who have done this before.

I'm not going to sugar-coat it. Becoming a Virgin Millionaire will take some serious work and not a small amount of time. Early on in your journey it may seem overwhelming and borderline impossible, but I promise you that with the right approach, some smart tactics and strategies and a consistent focus you can absolutely make it happen.

In each of the Smart Money Stages, there are seven focus areas: investing, saving, tax, property and debt, superannuation, risk and planning. In each of these seven areas there are key outcomes you need to achieve to 'complete' the stage and move on to the next.

It's important you complete each stage, because doing so means you've covered all the key areas. It's common for an investor to be doing well in one or a few areas, but to have left gaps in other areas. Trying to progress to the next stage *before* these gaps are addressed can result in serious trouble later on.

So one of the most important things you need to focus on if you want to truly nail it with your money is to achieve set milestones in every key financial focus area before you move on to the tactics and strategies of the next stage.

The Smart Money Stages and the outcomes you need to achieve to complete each stage are shown in table 1.1 (overleaf).

Your financial trajectory

As we talk through these stages, I'll refer to your financial trajectory. This is the pathway you're on now. As you move forward with your current rate of savings and investing, how much money will you have in a week, a year, 10 years? Everyone has a financial trajectory, but most don't understand it, which means they don't know where they're headed with their money

When you're clear on your financial trajectory, apart from getting a solid sense of how you're tracking, you'll be able to clearly understand whether what you're doing now is enough, too much or not enough to get you to where you want to be with your money, or when you will reach your target.

I'll unpack exactly how to map out your trajectory later, but for now I want to frame up the concept as it's an important element of your Smart Money Stages.

Foundations

The Foundations stage of your money, as the name suggests, involves setting up the building blocks of your future financial success. Because there is a significant gap between your current financial trajectory and where you want to end up, serious change will be required.

Table 1.1 Smart Money Stages: a progress tracker

	Investing	Tax	Saving & spending
IMPACT	Net investment income equal to double AU average income, w. income plan if employment ceased today	Multiple tax saving structures in place, including PAF	True ideal lifestyle spending while exceeding savings targets
ACCELERATE	Net investment income equal to AU average income	Be 100% confident you're not paying more than your fair share in tax, using multiple tax saving entities	10/10 satisfaction w. saving & spending - true 'ideal lifestyle' spending full achieved
OPTIMISE	Investing minimum 10% gross household income to shares	Investment strategy to include at least one tax structure outside of superannuation, e.g. bonds, trust, company etc.	9/10 satisfaction with saving & spending at current levels
FOCUS	Investing minimum 5% gross household income to shares	Leveraging multiple tax strategies to save a minimum $10k p.a. in tax	Saving and spending well and consistently
FOUNDATIONS	Have a regular investment plan for shares with automated weekly/monthly contributions	Leverage at least one strategy to save a minimum $1k p.a. tax	Be saving consistently each month to your savings plan with only minor deviations

	Property & debt	Superannuation	Risk	Planning
IMPACT	Deductible debt for property investments maximised in line with investment income plan. Own your dream home free of non ded. debt	At superannuation balance transfer cap	Be in a position to self insure against key financial risks	Complete financial freedom with true ideal lifestyle spending + surplus savings capacity
ACCELERATE	Own multiple investment properties with deductible debt maximised. Own your dream home free of non-deductible debt	On track to (at least) maximise superannuation balance transfer cap	Emergency fund at minimum 12 months living expenses	Be on track to exceed your financial freedom number within your desired timeframe
OPTIMISE	Own more than one quality investment property to support asset / wealth	Be fully using super contribution limits each year	Emergency fund at minimum six months living expenses. Personal insurance package in place	Be on track to reach your financial freedom number within your desired timeframe
FOCUS	Own (at least) one quality investment property	Be making some additional deductible contributions to super each year	Emergency fund at minimum three months living expenses	You have a clear plan and are consistently tracking to milestones you have set
FOUNDATIONS	Understanding the importance of property for wealth building	Superannuation consolidated and invested in line with a set investment strategy	Emergency fund in place	You're clear on your financial trajectory and have a plan to get there

What I've found is that you can't get out of the Foundations stage without making a commitment to your money. Money progress and money success won't just happen on their own. Money is one of those areas of life that's important but not urgent, so it's easy for life to get in the way of your investing the time and work needed to get your money progress on track.

When you lose focus on your money, it's easy for a day to turn into a week and then a month, and before you know it things have slipped to the point where you can be in a serious pickle. If this happens it will take some work (and time) to turn things around. Your commitment is the key.

Focus

The next stage is Focus. This stage is defined by your making some progress, but it's slower than you want it to be. You have the ability to make some of the personal and lifestyle choices you want, but typically they will come at the expense of making the financial progress you want.

At this stage you're not experiencing the same level of stress that is common at the Foundations stage, but you have an overarching level of concern around your money and the niggling sense that things should be better than they are.

At the Focus stage there is often a smaller but meaningful gap between the financial trajectory you're on and where you really want to be. This means you can't live the lifestyle you want today *and* hit your future money targets.

Optimise

The Optimise stage is marked by some significant positive changes. You're starting to build solid momentum with your investing and your money. By the end of this stage you have got your money to a point where you're on track for smart money freedom in a timeframe you're happy with. But there is still work to be done as you follow your path to building your savings, investments and wealth to the level that will enable you to be financially free.

At the Optimise stage you start building some serious financial and investing momentum, and along with this comes a game-changing level of confidence and peace of mind.

You're not yet able to live your ideal lifestyle fully as you continue to prioritise saving money to invest and to keep your momentum building, but your satisfaction rating with both your spending and your saving levels will be 9 out of 10.

Accelerate

This stage is the last stop before you complete your Virgin Millionaire journey and achieve true smart money freedom. You'll begin to exceed your targets for achieving smart money freedom within the timeframe you chose. It's time to rebalance and achieve the spending capacity for your ideal lifestyle.

This doesn't mean you'll be spending more money just because you can. It means you'll have taken the time to figure out exactly how much money you'll need to live the lifestyle you really want, and you can now afford to do this while continuing to hit the savings and investing targets that will build your future investments and wealth to exactly the level you want.

Impact

The final stage of smart money freedom is Impact. You're still playing the same game but at a completely different level. By the end of the Impact stage you'll have fully achieved smart money freedom. If you're still working, it's out of choice, not need.

There are effectively no limits on the lifestyle choices you can make because you have more money than you need. You are completely carefree!

Your progression

As I've discussed, moving between the Smart Money Stages is a progression. Remember, wherever you're at right now, you are exactly where you need to be.

It's completely natural to want more, but know that smart money freedom is a big goal that takes work and time. The important thing is to focus on your progress through the five stages rather than fixating on where you are (or aren't) right now.

Smart money freedom is a journey as much as a destination, and the good news is there are some key strategies that will allow you to make it easier to accelerate your progress between stages.

The first step is to make a commitment to your money. This is the bare minimum to get you through the Foundations stage, but it's also necessary as you progress through the later stages.

The key to moving beyond the Foundations stage is to commit to ongoing action. In short, you need to do stuff. You need to set up that savings account, ditch your debt, be smarter with your tax planning, sort out your superannuation, start a regular investment plan, and take whatever other next steps will move your money forward.

Once again, money success doesn't just happen on its own: action is the key to results.

But there is no such thing as a set-and-forget money strategy. The world is moving too quickly, and a smart move today *won't* necessarily be the smartest thing you can do a year or two from now. Ongoing flexibility is crucial.

If the past few years have taught us anything it's that the rate of change worldwide is accelerating; this applies to the economy, interest rates, financial markets, property, investment markets, investment products, technology and everything else. And beyond what's going on externally, you yourself are constantly changing in terms of what you want, what's important to you and what's going on with your money.

The smartest moves for you depend on what's happening in all these areas, which is why progressing to the Optimise stage and beyond requires you not only to take action now but to keep taking smart action into the future.

Getting beyond the Optimise stage requires another big shift, and this is the factor that will move the dial most on your rate of financial progress. The key here is maximising every single opportunity available to you with the money you have.

Squeezing every drop of juice out of your money will involve optimising your money and investments from a tax perspective and acquiring the best financial products at the lowest cost. You will need to have the right debt strategy and debt products in place and to optimise your investment and superannuation contribution strategies.

There are many different elements and aspects to your money and investments, from your banking and saving, investing, tax planning, property, superannuation and retirement account investing, risk management and debt. Getting the most out of each of these areas of your money is what will drive the rapid acceleration of your financial progress, and is *the* thing that pushes through the Optimise stage to Accelerate and Impact your achievement of true smart money freedom.

Pro tip: Maximising every opportunity is something you can start doing today—like right now—no matter which of the smart money freedom stages you're sitting in. If you're at one of the earlier stages, starting to maximise every opportunity now will greatly accelerate your progress through the stages.

The right move at the wrong time is the wrong move

One of the common ways people go wrong when trying to get ahead with their money is choosing the wrong time to make a money move. Timing causes a lot of confusion and frustration around money simply because people don't realise that the right move at the wrong time is the wrong move.

When most people talk about doing things with your money, they talk in absolute terms: buying shares is a good idea; you should buy your first property asap; contributing to super is a smart move, and so on.

The reality is that each of these things can be a great idea at one smart money stage and a complete disaster at a different stage. I've come to realise that which of these stages you're currently in dictates the approach you should be taking, which things make good sense and which do not.

This is why it's so important that you understand the Smart Money Stages and use this knowledge to guide your decision making. Without it, you can end up doing something that might be great for you in the future but a disaster for you today.

Ultimately the very best decision for you depends on you and your money, but there are some common success principles you can apply at each smart money stage.

Below I've listed some of the various financial focus projects you might work on as you progress through the Smart Money Stages. Along the way, other options begin to make more sense.

You should also know that it doesn't make sense to undertake some projects early, either because they will have less of an impact, or in some cases because they can lead to serious trouble.

Table 1.2 (overleaf) lists some of the financial focus projects that make sense at each smart money stage. You can see that these projects change throughout the Smart Money Stages. The reality is that while a project from one of the more advanced stages may be a 'good' idea, it won't have the same level of impact that it could (or should) have when you get the timing right. Further, some of the projects can actually slow your rate of progress if they're done at the wrong time — a disaster you'll want to avoid if you are to make maximum progress in the minimum amount of time.

Your focus through the Smart Money Stages

There is no one right set of tactics that will work for every person and situation, but there are some principles you should follow if getting ahead is important to you. Here I'll discuss the most important financial focus areas as you progress through the Smart Money Stages.

Smart Money Stage 1: Foundations

Your main focus at the Foundations stage should be on minimising your spending so you can build savings and eliminate any bad debt. A second strong focus should be on increasing your income in the short term to increase your savings capacity and accelerate your progress.

Two further key areas are building good money habits and systemising your approach to managing your money, savings and investments.

Bigger lifestyle spending should be eliminated entirely until you break out of the Foundations stage, or at least restricted to the bare minimum needed to keep you sane as you work your way through this stage.

Table 1.2 financial focus projects

	Investing	Tax	Saving & spending
IMPACT	Legacy investing roadmap	PAF legacy planning	The give back spending plan
ACCELERATE	Values & ethics investing plan	Tax entity optimisation	Income opt-out plan
	Sexy investing system	Tax accrual planning	'Ideal lifestyle' spending plan
OPTIMISE	The ETF accelerator	Introduction to tax structures	Income optimiser planning
	Investing structure game plan	Investment bond planning	Banking buckets
FOCUS	Investment philosophy 101	Superannuation	Income increaser
	Invest like Warren Buffet	Minimising your ATO donation	Conscious spending & saving plan
FOUNDATIONS	The automatic investing plan	Maximise your tax refund	Ditch your bad debt for good
	Micro investing mastery	Understanding AU tax rules	Spending & savings plan

Stage	Property & debt	Superannuation	Risk	Planning
IMPACT	Your private banker	Private super plan	Self insurance strategies	Intergenerational wealth roadmap
ACCELERATE	Optimising debt products	Introduction to SMSF strategies	Lifestyle risk eliminator	Family financial freedom planning
ACCELERATE	Deductible debt maximiser	Super balance cap maximiser	Insurance wind-back	Investment income optimisation
OPTIMISE	Mortgage rate sharpener	Catch-up contribution planner	Avoiding forced investment sales	Money decision making mastery
OPTIMISE	Property Buyers Agent	Super contributions maximiser	Optimising personal protection	Lifestyle risk planning
FOCUS	Build your money dream team	Deductible contributions 101	Personal insurance 101	Money progress tracker
FOCUS	Property deposit roadmap	Superannuation success strategies	Cost of the unexpected game plan	Smart Money Freedom number
FOUNDATIONS	First property plan	Super fund consolidation	Avoiding	Systemising planning success
FOUNDATIONS	FHB benefits 101	Superannuation 101	Emergency fund builder	Mapping your money trajectory

You should also focus on setting up a small, regular investment plan. This might be as little as $5 a week to start, which will allow you to build your investing knowledge and skills. From there you will be able to increase how much you're investing in order to start building some real money momentum.

Practically, you need to put together a budget, and start setting up your banking to make your money management and saving easier. This ties into building good habits around your money, because how you spend and save your money are the foundation for your ongoing money habits. It's also a big part of systemising your money.

Your money systems

You may not think too much about how you manage savings and investments or how you make money decisions, plan with your money or review your progress. But money systems go a long way towards driving your success.

My favourite quote from James Clear's blockbuster book, *Atomic Habits* is this: 'You don't rise to the level of your goals. You fall to the level of your systems.' This holds true in many important areas of life, but nowhere more than in those that involve your money.

This is because money is one of those things that's important but not urgent, and because we're generally time-poor. Often the easiest thing to do with money will deliver the opposite of money success.

Spending in the moment feels better than saving for tomorrow. Not taking the time to be organised and prepared throughout the year to stay on top of your taxes seems harder than just dealing with it after the end of the financial year. And not doing your monthly Smart Money Review (more on this later) and pulling yourself into line when things start getting off track can seem harder than just letting the good times roll.

Systems are important, because they provide structure that supports your money success. Your savings system will automate the results you want, and give you a clear feedback loop if you lose your focus.

Your monthly Smart Money Review forces you to celebrate your progress and build motivation, and to learn from any missteps or mistakes. And your annual planning session will keep you on top of your financial products and ensure you're getting the most out of your money. I'll unpack these systems in detail later, but for now just know they are important and highly valuable, and that they should be a critical focus to help you create a solid foundation for your long-term smart money freedom.

The Foundations stage is challenging and progressing through it will take hard work, sacrifice and focus. But the only way out is up, and the sooner you make it happen, the sooner you can be reflecting on the challenges of this stage from the comfort of the other side.

Increasing your income

Controlling your spending is powerful and important, but there's a limit to how much you can cut back on spending. There's no limit on how much you can increase your income.

When people think about getting ahead with money, they often overlook increasing income.

Even when you're earning a good income it's challenging to achieve smart money freedom in the timeframe you want—but without enough income it's almost impossible.

No matter which stage you're currently in, earning more income will help you progress faster. You absolutely should be considering how you can increase your income today and into the future.

There are two ways of increasing your work-related income. You can take on more work, by working extra hours in your current job or picking up gig work such as Uber driving or starting a side hustle.

The second and potentially more powerful way to increase your income is by changing jobs, careers or industries, or upskilling or reskilling with a view to receiving pay rises or promotions that come with a significantly higher income. This path will often take more time, but will likely drive a larger increase in your income.

Either option can work, but only you know whether and how they might work for you. Increasing your income isn't possible for absolutely everyone, but to be honest it is for most people, and if you don't have some focus on increasing your income it will take you a lot longer to achieve your smart money freedom.

Smart Money Stage 2: Focus

At this stage one of the key defining characteristics is that there is a gap between your current financial trajectory and the one you want to be on. This means you can't yet afford to live your ideal lifestyle *and* make the progress you want towards smart money freedom in a timeframe you're happy with.

At the Focus stage, you have more money available to you that you could spend, but doing so will increase the gap between where you are now and where you want to be. At this stage you'll benefit from keeping a strong focus on closing this gap *before* you ramp up spending.

There are only four ways you can close the gap: by saving more (spending less, earning more or both), investing more, using more (good) debt to invest more money sooner and paying less tax.

Your big goal at the Focus stage is to buy your first investment property, and I can't overstate the importance of this decision. We're going to dive deeper into this in later chapters, but the introduction of leverage (debt) into your investment strategy is a game changer, because you're combining your savings with the bank's money to acquire a much bigger investment than you could make on your own.

Once you have a good investment property behind you, you will benefit from a rising property market and create equity that can be used to invest more money in the future. The one move of buying your first property (when you get it right) will itself make you a bunch of money, but will also unlock your ability to make some crucial future moves that will make you even more.

You really do need to get your first property decision right. And before you start stressing, don't worry. I've got you covered. I'm going to help you understand exactly what you need to know to nail your first property purchase and use it to lay the platform for your future financial success.

Your first property purchase is likely to take some time, so your focus early on at this stage should be on increasing your regular investments in shares to get you to your goal sooner.

Risk management is crucial at this stage, both in your planning around investments—and specifically property investments—and in choosing quality investments that will deliver consistent growth into the future. I'll cover these in detail later.

Robust planning is your friend at the Focus stage. You need to be crystal clear on your trajectory, and to be moving forward methodically and consistently.

Then as you make your money and investing moves, you should be assessing the impact of any changes. Whether they're around spending, income, investing or debt, you should be looking not just at the short term but also at how changes you make now will impact your trajectory in the years ahead. This means you'll be well placed to make the smartest decisions for you and get the best results possible with the money you have today.

Skipping Smart Money Stages

It's common for people to start focusing on their money only once they are a little way along on their journey. You may have been tracking along for a while, doing okay with building savings and investments. Maybe you have even bought a property. Then you come to the realisation that a shift in your approach is needed to get to where you really want to be.

First, well done on coming to that realisation. Lots of people fall into the good-enough trap with money once they've got a bit going on. You figure that because you have a decent income, a few bucks in your savings account and some investments, you're doing well enough.

This approach is costly, first because, as I've discussed, smart money freedom doesn't happen without your maintaining a clear focus and making the right moves at the right times. What people in the good-enough trap don't realise is that every week or month they delay is a cost that can never be recovered.

Second, it's important you know that regardless of where you're at when you begin your Virgin Millionaire journey, you must complete each stage before you move on to the next. If you've already got some good things in place with your money, your progress should be a lot faster. But you should still work through each smart money stage and ensure every element is completed before you move on.

The very real risk is that you'll leave a gap that will cost you dearly when you get into more advanced territory.

Smart Money Stage 3: Optimise

At the Optimise stage, you're building some solid money momentum and seeing the real benefits of the work you've done to date. And you're getting a taste of the freedom and confidence that will continue building into the later stages.

This stage has one chunky goal: to get your savings and investments on track to achieve smart money freedom in the timeframe you've set.

As I've pointed out, there are just four ways you can close the gap and speed up your financial trajectory: earning more or spending less (or both), investing more of your cash savings, using more leverage or debt, and paying less tax. At the Optimise stage, you will need to consider which of these options, or which combination of options, will work best for you—and then make it happen.

At this stage you'll also acquire your second investment property. This may be the second most important investment you'll ever make. As with your first property purchase, it will benefit you in the short term and further ahead, because you will choose a property whose value will increase, it will result in more equity for future investing.

As you introduce more debt into your investment strategy, risk management becomes all-important. You'll benefit from careful and considered planning. At this point, if you haven't already built your dream team of professionals to support you with investing and asset building, now is the time to do so.

Smart tax planning is another important focus area at the Optimise stage. It's where you'll introduce your first non-superannuation tax entity for investing—another big decision that will have a significant payoff when you get it right.

Smart Money Stage 4: Accelerate

You come into the Accelerate stage on track to achieve smart money freedom in your chosen timeframe, so while there's still work to be done, the focus shifts again, this time to creating your ideal lifestyle.

The risk at this stage is that you'll become distracted and wander off track. You may start spending too much or slow down your investing so that you end up falling short of the smart money freedom you've planned. It goes without saying this scenario should be avoided at all costs.

The first thing you'll want to do is crank up your investing so you start to exceed your smart money freedom targets. This in turn will allow you to increase spending while remaining on track. At the Accelerate stage you'll work through an iterative process until you're spending at your ideal lifestyle level while remaining on track to exceed your targets.

At this stage it's important you keep a clear focus on managing risk. You come into this stage already on track to achieve your money goals and then look to ramp up your financial trajectory even further, so the biggest risk at this stage is that something throws you off track.

It's crucial that your emergency fund is sufficient to cover any cashflow risk, that you're effectively protected with personal insurances such as income replacement, and that your investment choices are rock solid to deliver consistent returns into the future while avoiding downside risk.

From a planning and spending perspective, the fun really starts at this stage. Take the time now to review your ideal lifestyle spending targets to make sure your investments will truly cover your version of ideal.

Smart Money Stage 5: Impact

Completing the impact stage means you've made it. Your wealth is such that you need never work again. This is exactly where you want to be. You've put in the work needed to fully achieve your version of smart money freedom, and now it's time to celebrate.

Don't get me wrong. There will still be work involved in managing all the moving parts of the serious money machine you've created.

An important focus now is ensuring your existing money and investments are still working to their full potential. At the Impact stage you'll find there are points where you can invest more without taking on excessive extra risk, use smart debt to create more upside and optimise your tax structuring to get more out of the money you have. You'll have peace of mind knowing your money is working to its full potential.

The 5 per cent rule unpacked

If you're young you're probably not thinking too much about retirement, but the latest statistics released from the ATO (2021) show that in Australia the average retiree income is less than $20k—around 21 per cent of the average income of a full-time worker.

Based on these figures, the reality is that most people will have to drastically cut costs and make considerable lifestyle sacrifices in their later years, a pretty frightening prospect for many people. But with the right approach this predicament is avoidable.

When it comes to money and investing, the 5 per cent rule will help you figure out exactly how much money you will need in the future to live your ideal lifestyle. This will help you set money targets and get clear on how your financial trajectory is tracking relative to your goals.

The 5 per cent rule says that you can generate an income of around 5 per cent from investments each year without eating into your capital (reducing your balance). So, for example, if you have $1 million invested you should be able to derive an income of around $50k each year for the rest of your life.

This is based on long-term returns on investments of 9.8 per cent. After allowing for fees and inflation, you're left with 5 per cent. The 'rule' is a rough estimate and although it isn't perfect, it's generally dependable enough to help you set some solid money targets.

Knowing how much income your investments can generate in turn allows you to calculate how much you need to have in investments to achieve smart money freedom.

The final piece of the puzzle you will need to set a clear target is how much income you want or need in the future. This is your smart money freedom income.

Setting targets will help you understand exactly where you want to get to, and to be clear on how big your smart money freedom gap is. To use this rule to set your targets, think about what your ideal level of income for the future would be.

I get that retirement can seem a long way away and it can be hard to figure out what the right number might be. You'll do some more work on this number through the book and over time, but you don't want to get stuck at this point. Your current income level is a good place to start.

Once you have your income target number, simply divide the number by 5 per cent to get your investment balance target.

For example, if you want an annual investment income of $100k, you can use the 5 per cent rule as follows:

$$\$100\,000 / 5\% = \$2\,000\,000$$

To achieve an income in the future of $100k a year, you'll need to have around $2 million in investments, so this becomes your target. It would give you an annual retirement income around $80k more than that of today's average.

Note that your smart money freedom income will tell you how much money you need to have in investments, not including your home. While your home is an asset, and some would consider it an investment, it won't make you any money until you sell it. So your true smart money freedom target is how much you will need in investments exclusive of the value of your home. I'll get into this in a heap more detail later, but for now I want to plant the seed of this reality.

Table 1.3 presents a simple tracker to help you calculate your net asset position today. The figures in the second column offer an example.

You can see from this example that the overall net asset position is $455 000, but when your own home is excluded the net asset value is actually negative. This is common for homeowners and shouldn't throw you off. As explained, your home is excluded from your investment assets because it doesn't provide an income. However, the debt needs to be included because it will need to be repaid eventually.

Table 1.3 calculating your net asset position

Category	Value ($)
Cash savings	18000
Share investments	22000
Sexy investments (e.g. crypto, gold)	–
Own home value	850000
Own home mortgage	570000
Investment property	–
Investment property mortgage	–
Superannuation	135000
Total net assets today	455000
Total net assets excluding home	–395000

Apply this to your current financial position to quantify your smart money freedom gap—that is, how much more money you'd need today to be completely financially free (table 1.4).

Table 1.4 calculating your smart money freedom gap

Category	Value ($)
Net investments target ($100k @ 5%)	2000000
Dream home target	850000
Smart money freedom target (investment + home value)	2850000
Total net assets	455000
Smart money freedom gap	2395000

You can use these simple trackers as a starting point to get a solid sense of where you are today, where you want to take your money and the gap reflecting the work to be done. Becoming clear on this is an important step in framing your thinking to start your Virgin Millionaire journey, and is something you should refer back to regularly as you proceed. We've also put together a spreadsheet version of this you can download free at bit.ly/virginmillionaire or from the Pivot Wealth website.

You have to get started—now

It should go without saying, but just to say it: once you know where you want to end up, the next step is to start planning to get there.

If you're still early in your money journey, there's probably a big gap between where you are today and where you want to get to. But don't stress. As I pointed out in the Introduction, most people underestimate the power of compound interest over time.

Table 1.5 shows how much you need to save and invest daily, based on your age and your smart money freedom target.

Table 1.5 how much you need to save to build different levels of wealth

		Age							
		20	25	30	35	40	45	50	55
Daily saving to build wealth by age 65	$1m investments ($50k income)	$3.32	$5.49	$9.04	$15.06	$25.41	$44.05	$80.12	$161.03
	$1.5m investments ($75k income)	$4.98	$8.24	$13.56	$22.59	$38.12	$66.08	$120.18	$241.55
	$2m investments ($100k income)	$6.64	$10.98	$18.08	$30.12	$50.83	$88.11	$160.24	$322.06
	$2.5m investments ($125k income)	$8.30	$13.73	$22.60	$37.64	$63.53	$110.14	$200.30	$402.58
	$3m investments ($150k income)	$9.96	$16.47	$27.12	$45.17	$76.24	$132.16	$240.36	$483.09
	$4m investments ($200k income)	$13.28	$21.96	$36.16	$60.23	$101.65	$176.22	$320.48	$644.12
	$5m investments ($250k income)	$16.60	$27.45	$45.21	$75.29	$127.07	$220.27	$400.60	$805.15

Using this example, if your investment target is $2 million and you're 20 years old today, you would need to save and invest only $6.64 each day to hit your target by age 65.

But as you now know, the longer you leave it, the more work you need to do. If you wait until you're 30, 40 or 50, you will need to save and invest $18.08, $50.83 or a whopping $160.24 a day to achieve the same result.

With time on your side, you don't need to save a huge amount of money to hit a pretty solid target. Six dollars is about the cost of an extra shot hazelnut latte at your favourite café, so it should be achievable for most people; $18 a day will be harder but probably also doable. Almost $50 a day, let alone $160 a day, is going to get pretty challenging.

Leverage is the hidden accelerator

You can see from the table 1.3 that consistent saving and investing over the long term will drive some pretty epic investment- and wealth-building outcomes, but it gets better. Leverage or good investment debt is an accelerator that will grow wealth even faster than outlined in the table. As I've outlined, this is because when you borrow money in order to invest it, you combine the bank's money with yours to invest more than you could were you to rely on your savings alone.

Chapter 2 is dedicated to debt and how you can use smart debt to progress faster, but for now just know that even if you're falling slightly (or more than slightly) short of your ideal targets based on the numbers above, you do have a lever you can use to drive greater progress.

Money milestones

Getting to smart money freedom is no small feat. It will take serious focus and time—perhaps years, even decades. The good news is that when you follow the Virgin Millionaire process, you're going to enjoy the journey just as much as the destination.

I believe that financial freedom should be fairly high on your list of priorities, but it may not be the most important thing in your life.

In my opinion, it's important you enjoy your lifestyle today and in the years ahead, before you hit true financial freedom. A bad outcome is spending years (or decades) of your life not enjoying yourself so you can save and invest more money, only to become financially free a few years sooner.

I don't think spending is the key to happiness, or that you shouldn't ruthlessly cut your spending on things that you don't really value. But one of my big criticisms of some widely accepted approaches to money, such as FI/RE (financial independence, retire early) and others, is their emphasis on hitting savings and investment numbers at the cost of being happy with the way you're living today. Just like fad diets and intensive fitness challenges, some investment strategies prove unsustainable over the long term.

In this chapter, I've spoken a lot about setting targets, and pushing through the Smart Money Stages, but I want to make sure you focus on two important things: sustainable spending and celebrating money milestones.

Sustainable spending

First, spend on the things that are really important, things that really give you pleasure, and factor them into your plan. The stage you're at will dictate the best way to approach this.

Ruthlessly cut spending on anything that's not truly important to you. If you're currently at the Foundations stage, delay your important but not absolutely necessary spending as much as possible. The more you spend, the longer you'll be stuck at the Foundations stage. Often, though, just knowing you'll soon be able to spend more will encourage you to push forward to get to the next stage asap.

If you're at the Focus stage, think about the highest priority spending and factor in some of this, again bearing in mind that the more spending you can delay or avoid altogether, the faster you'll make it to the next stage. Aim to set up your spending in a way you're comfortable with for the medium term.

When you reach the Optimise stage, your money will be building its own momentum and this will take some of the pressure off your spending and saving. As a result, by the end of this stage you'll be at a nine-out-of-ten level of satisfaction with your spending and savings balance.

Cracking into the Accelerate stage you're on track to achieve smart money freedom, and you'll be aiming to build on your goal. You can now increase spending to the level needed to fund your true ideal lifestyle, a pretty epic place to be at.

Finally, at the Impact stage, you've fully achieved smart money freedom, and you still have a surplus of income beyond your ideal level of spending. The sky's the limit (almost), so you should think through any spending you now want to make possible. Don't go crazy and spend more than your investments are generating, but if you increase spending and you're still in surplus, then game on.

Celebrating money milestones

The second element is about ensuring that you have clear money milestones mapped out, and that you celebrate them. This is the seriously fun part.

I suggest you should be celebrating even as you make good progress towards your smart money freedom milestones. Because your final goal will take some time to reach, money milestone celebrations will help break down the big target into bite-sized chunks.

You then have a short-term target and can focus on exactly what you need to do to get there. When you hit that milestone, celebrate and recognise the progress you've made. This will motivate you to keep moving forward and nail the next milestone.

There are two solid ways you can set your money milestone targets, one based on the total value of your savings and investments, and the other based on your rate of progress towards your smart money freedom number.

The first is probably the simplest, and the best. You set your targets based on a dollar figure in savings or investments. For example, you might set your first money milestone at building $50k in savings, another at having $100k in your share portfolio, and then increase your targets from there.

The second is to look at how far you are along the path to smart money freedom. For example, if your target is $2 million, then once you have built $100k in wealth you'll be 5 per cent of the way towards your goal. With $200k in wealth you'll be 10 per cent of the way along, and so on, until you eventually reach 100 per cent—and go beyond it.

Each approach has advantages and disadvantages, and the right way to set *your* money milestones is the one that makes the most sense to you. Because you want this to be as simple and clear as possible both to understand and to track, I recommend the dollar-based method, but if you're a percentages person then go for the second method. Either way, setting money milestones will give you a clear target to aim for, which means you can employ a laser focus to get there.

One important thing to call out here is that your money milestone targets should be set so they can be achieved within the next 12 months—*this is non-negotiable*. This enables a crystal-clear short-term focus at the same time as it breaks down big goals into manageable chunks. As the saying goes, the best way to eat an elephant is one bite at a time.

Now you have your targets set, spend some time planning the celebration that will be your reward for hitting your milestone. It doesn't need to be lavish or ultra-expensive, but it does need to be something you *really* want, something that gets you excited, so when you're putting in the work to get there you'll have something positive to focus on other than just having more money.

In the earlier stages when you have less money, your reward can be something as modest as cooking up your favourite meal at home, taking an extra long weekend off work or enjoying a meal out at your favourite restaurant.

As your money momentum builds you will have the flexibility to upgrade your milestone celebrations. It may be a holiday to a place you've always wanted to visit, something for your house, a new car, a tech toy, a watch or a handbag—whatever gets you pumped.

Spending on more expensive things isn't mandatory, and if you're not into this sort of stuff don't feel compelled to spend money for the sake of it. But if there's an experience or thing you really want that fits into your savings and investment plan, feel comfortable about celebrating your progress.

When you do your money milestone targets well, you'll be more motivated to smash your goals sooner, and make faster progress. And you'll enjoy some clear and impactful celebrations along the way.

THE WRAP

Most of the people I speak to about their money tell me how important it is for them to get ahead *and* live a good lifestyle today. But the statistics show us that we're not getting the balance right. Most people aren't putting away enough for the future, which means they're enjoying today but will be forced to make drastic sacrifices in the future. This is my worst nightmare and something I think you should want to avoid at all costs.

We've considered five clearly defined stages people go through on their Virgin Millionaire journey. These stages take you from just getting started all the way through to full smart money freedom. Your progress through these stages reflects a levelling up of your money, and increased flexibility around your lifestyle and spending.

There's a simple formula to progress through the stages faster and more easily. But simple doesn't mean easy, and negotiating the five stages will take time and work. Understanding these stages is the first step, and once you know the best approach to take to reach the next level, your focus will become clear.

(continued)

The right move at the wrong time is the wrong move, and which stage you're at right now will dictate the approach you should take, and which money moves make sense for you, and which don't.

The next steps you'll take to achieve smart money freedom is to get clear on your targets, specifically how much money you'll need to have in investments to achieve true freedom. This means you'll be crystal clear on where you want to get to, and from there you will be able to break down your big goal into smaller, more manageable ones. The final step is to set some milestone celebrations that will get you pumped up to start smashing new targets.

Achieving smart money freedom is a big deal and will take serious effort and time. But on the journey you'll have confidence that your money is heading to a place you're excited by, where you'll find peace of mind and a more enjoyable future. Further, when you work through the smart money freedom stages and bake in some quality celebrations along the way, you'll enjoy the journey as much as the destination.

Take action

- Read and re-read the section on the Smart Money Stages until you're crystal clear on the fact you need to make the right moves for the stage you're currently at with your money.

- Use the tracker in table 1.1 to assess which Smart Money Stage you're currently in.

- Start thinking about your ideal lifestyle spending target and how much you'd want to spend on your dream home.

- Create your draft smart money freedom number.

- Map out your current financial position using the tracker template in table 1.1.

- Calculate your smart money freedom target so you know what you're aiming for.

- Calculate your current smart money freedom gap.

- Workshop a list of 'money milestone' celebrations. Start small but also think big.

CHAPTER 2

You need debt to get rich

Borrowing to invest allows you to use the bank's money to get ahead, which can fast-track your progress to smart money freedom. You can get there without debt, but your progress will be slower going and harder fought.

I find that most people I talk to about money and investing are risk conscious. It's natural and smart to worry about taking a costly misstep that will set you back. There are lots of ways to be right when it comes to money and investing, and ultimately the right strategy for you is the one you're comfortable with. As excited as I sometimes get when helping people build a financial plan, I fully recognise and appreciate that how you follow through is what will drive outcomes and results.

If you include something in your money plan just because someone says it's a good idea, but you don't have the confidence to act on it, then even if it's the best plan it won't work for you.

That said, I want to make my position on debt clear. You can get ahead and become a Virgin Millionaire without using debt, but in my opinion it just doesn't make sense. It will take a lot longer, and you'll simply be leaving too much money on the table.

Don't get me wrong, I recognise that borrowing money comes with risks that are important to manage. But these risks can be managed well, and when you use debt the smart way you will reach smart money freedom a lot faster. Later in this chapter I'll cover the key risks that come with borrowing money to invest and how these risks can be managed effectively.

There are two big reasons why using smart debt as part of your investment strategy should be on your radar.

Smart debt accelerates your wealth building

When you borrow money to invest, you end up with more investments than you could build with your savings alone. This means more investments growing for you, and therefore more investment profits.

Say, for example, you have $100 000 saved and you're considering whether to invest in shares or property. If you were to invest the money in shares, based on the long-term share market return of 9.8 per cent, your expected return would be $9800 over the next 12 months.

If instead you were to use the $100 000 as a deposit and borrow funds to buy a $500 000 property, your expected return based on the long-term property growth rate of 6.3 per cent would be $31 500 ($500k × 6.3 per cent). On top of this growth return, you receive rental income, which makes the total return from your property investment even higher.

By investing with debt into property, your annual investment return from the same money is $21 700 higher. Further, although the long-term return on property is slightly lower, your absolute return will be higher because your investment is five times as large ($500k vs $100k).

Smart debt gives you tax breaks

On top of the benefit of debt mentioned above, under the tax rules in Australia there's another serious upside of using debt to invest. Any time you use borrowed money to invest, all your borrowing costs are tax deductible, so you get to invest more and cut your tax bill at the same time.

After-tax borrowing rate for property investing

Because interest costs are tax deductible, the after-tax cost of your borrowing is reduced. You can calculate your after-tax interest rate using this formula:

$$\text{After-tax interest rate} = \text{before-tax interest rate} \times (1 - \text{marginal tax rate})$$

Let's use some real numbers. If you take out a bank mortgage with a headline interest rate of 6 per cent and your marginal tax rate + Medicare levy is 32 per cent (based on an income above $45k p.a.), your after-tax interest rate will be:

$$\text{After-tax interest rate} = 6\% \times (100\% - 32\%)$$
$$= 4.08\%$$

If your marginal tax rate is higher, it gets even better. If you're on the top marginal tax rate of 47 per cent, your after-tax interest rate will be:

$$\text{After-tax interest rate} = 6\% \times (100\% - 47\%)$$
$$= 3.18\%$$

You can see from these figures that your after-tax borrowing costs are between 2 and 3 per cent lower than the headline interest rate, and that the real after-tax cost of borrowing is between ~3 and 4 per cent.

What this means is that so long as any investment you make with these borrowed funds returns *more* than the after-tax interest rate (3.18%–4.08%) you're making money.

When your borrowing costs are lower, your investment will make you more money after costs and tax, which is the only return that matters when planning your wealth-building strategy.

Here's an example of the upside of borrowing to invest in property, based on the long-term return on the property market of 6.3 per cent.

If you were to buy a $1 million property, the expected growth based on the long-term return of 6.3 per cent will average out at $63 000 annually. The rental income will be around 3.71 per cent of the property value (current Australian average at the time of writing), adding another $37 100k p.a. to your total investment return.

If you were to borrow to purchase this property based on the after-tax interest rate of 4.2 per cent, your annual borrowing costs would be $42 000. This is worth noting as property ownership comes with ongoing costs like council or strata rates, insurances and so on. These costs average out at around 1 per cent of the value of a property, so on a $1 million property ongoing annual costs would be around $10 000.

This means your total return after borrowing will be $63 000 (growth) + $37 100 (rental income) – $42 000 (debt costs) – $10 000 (ongoing property costs), delivering you an annual upside profit of $48 100.

The numbers are compelling.

In the early stages of your Virgin Millionaire journey, funding your first property investments will be a challenge. You'll need to build up savings and savings capacity and carefully manage your risk. But think about what this will look like in the later stages, when you have not only heaps of money behind you but also property investments, solid property equity and strong savings capacity.

You can get tens of thousands of dollars (or hundreds of thousands of dollars) of essentially free money by using the bank's money for your own investments. This may sound too good to be true, but I'm not talking about some Airbnb or dropshipping strategy that has you doing this within a matter of months. This will take years of work and focus, but it is completely achievable for anyone prepared to follow the Virgin Millionaire approach.

How to use debt

Property investment is the most common way debt is used to grow wealth in Australia (and around the world), but it's not your only option.

You can borrow to invest in anything. The second most common debt-funded investment is shares, but you could also use debt to invest in businesses, crypto, artwork, collectibles and so on. The only real limits here are your imagination and risk tolerance.

The reason property is the most common debt-funded investment is because it's the investment banks are most comfortable to lend against, which means you'll be able to borrow more money at lower interest rates. And because the banks are the ones lending you the money, their comfort levels are important.

The banks understand the property market through the long-term history of values and performance. They know which states and suburbs involve more and less risk and they use this knowledge to assess borrowing capacity and levels. And since they are able to secure their interest in your property investment, they are more inclined to lend.

To sum up, not only are banks more comfortable lending you more money for investing in property than for other types of investment but the interest rate is generally much lower.

After-tax borrowing rate for share investing

The average variable mortgage interest rate in Australia in March 2024 was 6.98 per cent. The average rate for an unsecured loan is 10.63 per cent, and the average interest rate for a share-investing margin loan is over 10 per cent.

You can see from these figures that it's significantly more expensive to borrow for anything other than property. Again, it's important to look at the after-tax borrowing rate on this tax-deductible investment debt. Here I've included this formula using the higher interest rate that would apply to non-property borrowing:

After-tax interest rate = before-tax interest rate × (1 − marginal tax rate)

Using the average interest rate for non-property borrowing of 10.63 per cent, and your marginal tax rate + Medicare levy is 32 per cent (on income earned above $45k p.a.), your after-tax interest rate will be:

$$\text{After-tax interest rate} = 10.63\% \times (100\% - 32\%)$$
$$= 7.23\%$$

If you are to make money from borrowing to invest, your after-tax investment return needs to be greater than the borrowing costs, in this case 7.23 per cent.

We can calculate the after-tax expected return using this formula:

After-tax return = before-tax return − tax at marginal rate

This is how things look using the long-term return on the share market of 9.8 per cent, and the same marginal tax rate of 30 per cent:

$$\text{After-tax return} = 9.8\% \times (100\% - 32\%)$$
$$= 6.66\%$$

In this example, the cost of borrowing is higher than the expected investment return, resulting in a loss. In simple terms, this isn't a good investment move.

We have just experienced one of the fastest interest-rate tightening cycles in a generation. Interest rates today are higher than long-term averages for the recent past, and as rates return to a more normal level it's likely the expected return from borrowing to invest in shares will become positive.

I'm a fan of smart borrowing, and I love the tax breaks that come with using debt to fund investments in the right circumstances. In my opinion, based on the high interest costs that come with borrowing to invest in shares and the associated risks, I think that borrowing at interest rates significantly higher than those that apply to a property mortgage isn't the smartest move for most people.

But if you really want to borrow to invest in shares or in something else other than property, don't think it's never going to be possible. Once you buy investment properties that grow in value the banks will lend money against them at property borrowing rates, and you can then invest in whatever is going to work best for you (more on this to follow).

I get a lot of questions from people who aren't quite ready or able to buy a property asking whether there's a good stepping-stone strategy that involves debt and investing before you buy your first property. Unfortunately I've yet to find one I think is a solid play.

If we're agreed that smart debt is a good path to wealth building, and if there isn't a good stepping-stone, borrow-to-invest strategy, this suggests to me the smartest move is to push yourself to get into the property market as soon as possible.

Investment property vs your own home

I'll be focusing on property in the next chapter, but for now I want to call out that for the rest of the chapter when I talk about buying property, and specifically about buying your first property, I'm referring to property as an investment rather than as your own home.

I will also dive deeper into the numbers around property. With the average property increasing in value by tens of thousands of dollars each year, it's in your interest to get onto the property ladder as quickly as possible. Once you're in the market you have property working for you and you can focus on your next investment move.

Property affordability is at historically low levels so I get that this isn't easy, but given how important it is for your long-term money success it's worth working for.

Investing and your property deposit

Pulling together the deposit for your first property is no small undertaking. It takes time to get there, and saving money in a bank account can be slow and frustrating. Your frustration may be amplified when you consider the impact of inflation on the value of your money.

Saving a deposit takes time and work, so you need to keep yourself motivated. As you start to build your deposit, consider how you can get this money working harder while you're saving.

Enter share investing. Directing your savings into shares should earn you a return higher than the rate of inflation. It also reduces the frustration you may feel over how long it's taking for your savings to grow large enough to become your property deposit.

You may be on track with your savings to have enough for your property deposit in one to two years, at which time you'll probably want to sell your shares and have the cash available.

What if you invest your savings in shares and just before you plan to buy your property there's a share market crash? It's not going to be a good idea to sell your shares. If you don't have to buy your property (which you don't), you can leave the money invested until the market recovers.

Consider investing more while markets are down, when you can pick up quality investments at a discount. Then all you need to do is wait for the recovery and you'll likely gain much more than you were initially expecting.

This would allow you to buy the same property with a bigger deposit and a lower mortgage, or a more expensive property, or to just leave the money invested to grow your wealth.

The key point here is that you don't *need* this money; you just want it. My take on this is that if you're in this position, even if the timeline you'd like to work towards is shorter, shares can be a good option.

The odds are in your favour. On average, Australian shares have gone backwards (lost money) in only four of the last 20 years. This suggests it's much more likely shares will go up than down, so you'll be able to buy your property when you want to. And you'll get to do it knowing that your money was working hard for you along the way.

It's not without risk, though. If buying a property in 18 months is really mission critical for you, then growth investments like shares probably aren't the right move.

Quality is critical

Early on in your Virgin Millionaire journey, it's going to take time to build the savings needed to make your first property purchase happen, but you want to get into the property market asap so you don't fall further behind.

That said, it's critical that your first property purchase is a good long-term investment. It has to make money, not least because in doing so it will unlock the equity to allow you to invest using the power of leverage.

To do this, your property *must* increase in value over time. If you buy a dud property that doesn't grow in value, you're going to be in a difficult position. Not only will you not make money on your investment, but you won't benefit from the equity increase that will enable further borrowing for investment. The property will consume your borrowing capacity, which will limit further investing.

If this happens, you will be faced with a difficult choice. Selling a property involves costs that you'll then need to recover, and buying a replacement involves a further set of costs. This is why it's so important to choose a good property, particularly in the early Smart Money Stages.

The good news is that choosing a property that will grow over the long term is relatively simple. In the following chapter I'll unpack exactly how to find a good property, but for now keep in mind that you're not likely to pick up a bargain if you're looking for a premium property in a premium area.

Given the high cost of premium houses, if you want to buy a quality property you're probably looking at an apartment in a premium area. In my opinion this is completely okay. You're likely to be much better off investing in a one-bedroom apartment for $500k in a strong growth area, than spending the same amount on a much bigger home in a lower-growth area.

While the past doesn't predict the future when it comes to investment returns, you can see this approach would have delivered for you at any time over the past hundred years, and I don't see anything to suggest the next hundred years will be much different.

So, when formulating your first-property game plan, you should get clear on the minimum amount you need to spend to get a quality property that will be a good long-term investment.

The next step is to speak to a mortgage broker or bank to understand your borrowing options. Even if your property purchase is a long way off, it's generally a good idea to start the conversation and research early.

A mortgage broker will be able to tell you what government schemes you can access and help you get clear on exactly how much you need to have in savings for a deposit. It's worth noting that this is a bit of a moving target because how banks assess borrowing ability changes over time, so what you'll need in six or twelve months' time may differ from what you need today.

But you can only plan with the information available to you today, and it's okay if your plan needs to be adjusted. At least you have something to follow, meaning you'll get there faster with less stress.

Mortgage broker or bank?

If you borrow to buy property, you'll need a mortgage. You can either go to the bank directly or use a mortgage broker to help you through the process. Both can work, but in my opinion a mortgage broker is the better option.

A mortgage broker can access a range of different banks and mortgage products and can typically find you a better interest rate, whereas the bank will be limited to offering you their own set of products. Mortgage brokers also help project manage the administration that comes with setting up a mortgage, which can save you time (and frustration).

More is more when investing in property

If you're on a strong path with your income and savings capacity, it's likely you either could already—or will very soon—be in a position to borrow to buy a property.

There are lots of different ways to be right when it comes to investing in property, and the right approach for you will depend on what matters to you. But in the later stages of smart money freedom, it will be helpful to maximise your property exposure (value of property investments) while minimising the number of properties you own.

The way I see it, each property you buy means more things to think about. More tenants, property managers, and bank and loan accounts, all of which will require some level of administration.

In my opinion, if your aim is to hold $2 million in investment properties, it would be better to hold two $1 million properties than four $500k properties. You will have fewer to manage, and a $1 million property is likely to have fewer vacancies and more stable tenants. You'll have the same degree of exposure to property and potentially a better overall return for less work. A big win in my book.

If you're in a stronger financial position, instead of rushing to buy the first property you can afford you may benefit from waiting (a little). You won't want to delay too long, but if a few months is going to make the difference between buying a $900k property and a $1.2 million property that will be a better long-term investment, a small delay may be smart.

Investing with equity

There are very few free rides when it comes to investing but investing with equity is as close as you can get. This is a strategy to focus on as soon as you own property and it's the next step if you're serious about becoming a Virgin Millionaire.

It's worth starting with the basics here. Property 'equity' is simply the difference between the value of your property and how much you owe on your mortgage. For example, if your property is worth $500k and you owe $300k, your 'equity' is $200k.

In Australia, the banks will comfortably lend you up to 80 per cent of the value of a property. You must be able to service the mortgage — that is, have a stable income and buy a property that will give you enough rent to cover the ongoing mortgage costs and so on. But assuming you can cover the mortgage repayments, from the bank's perspective borrowing should be relatively straightforward.

As the value of your first property purchase increases with time, so will your equity. You can then borrow against your equity and effectively invest without using your savings. You can use your savings to make other investments and seriously accelerate your wealth building.

How equity release works

This may seem complex but the short version is that as both your property value and your equity increase, the banks will be comfortable about lending you more.

You'll generally need a cash deposit to buy your first property. But once you have property equity, the banks will lend you money against it and you can use that money as the deposit for another property purchase.

This means you can buy your second and subsequent properties without using any cash savings or putting down any of your own money. You're using the bank's money to invest and build your assets, which is a big part of why property is a fast track to serious wealth. It's important if you choose to go down this path that you manage your risk well, and I'll explain exactly how you can do this shortly.

Table 2.1 illustrates how much you could potentially borrow based on the increasing value of your first property ($500k).

Table 2.1 how property equity grows over time

Years	0	1	2	3	4
Property $500k @ 6.3%	$500 000	$531 500	$564 985	$600 579	$638 415
Equity @ 80%	$400 000	$425 200	$451 988	$480 463	$510 732
Loan	$400 000	$400 000	$400 000	$400 000	$400 000
Borrowing available	$ 0	$ 25 200	$ 51 988	$ 80 463	$110 732

Years	5	10	20	30	40
Property $500k @ 6.3%	$678 635	$921 091	$1 696 818	$3 125 849	$5 758 384
Equity @ 80%	$542 908	$736 873	$1 357 455	$2 500 679	$4 606 707
Loan	$400 000	$400 000	$ 400 000	$ 400 000	$ 400 000
Borrowing available	$142 908	$336 873	$ 957 455	$2 100 679	$4 206 707

Family guarantee

Table 2.2 outlines how equity release can work to help you buy a property. The family guarantee works in the same way, with the one big difference—instead of using the equity in your property as a deposit, you use the equity in a family member's property.

It's natural to feel nervous about a family guarantee, and this stops many people from pursuing this as an option. But in reality the biggest risk is that you choose not to make your mortgage repayments, which can be avoided with smart planning around your property purchase.

(continued)

If your parents (or other family members) own a property with some equity and you think accessing it might be possible for you, I'd strongly suggest seeking out a good professional to help you understand how a family guarantee could work for you.

This strategy could help you buy your first property sooner or buy a property with a higher value than you could otherwise afford.

It's not for everyone, but if it works for you (and for your family) it can get you onto the property ladder a lot sooner. If you think this strategy might be right for you, I suggest educating yourself and getting some good advice.

In the early years, the growth in equity is slower because you're starting from a lower base, but with compounding, over time both property value and equity accelerate.

The example in table 2.2 is based on investing in a second property. Note that $500k is way below the Australian median property value of $956 782, and that we're only using two properties, so there is potential for your results to be significantly stronger.

Table 2.2 how equity increases your borrowing ability

Year	1	2	3	4	5
Property $500k @ 6.3%	**$531 500**	**$564 985**	**$600 579**	$ 638 415	$ 678 635
Equity @ 80%	$ 425 200	$ 451 988	$ 480 463	$ 510 732	$ 542 908
Loan	$ 400 000	$ 400 000	$ 400 000	$ 400 000	$ 400 000
Borrowing available	$ 25 200	$ 51 988	$ 80 463	$ 110 732	$ 142 908
Property 2 @ $500k	$ 0	$ 0	$ 0	$ 500 000	$ 531 500
Property 2 loan	$ 0	$ 0	$ 0	$ 500 000	$ 500 000
Property 2 equity	$ 0	$ 0	$ 0	$ 0	$ 31 500
Total assets	**$531 500**	**$564 985**	**$600 579**	**$1 138 415**	**$1 210 135**
Total debt	$ 400 000	$ 400 000	$ 400 000	$ 900 000	$ 900 000
Total wealth (assets – debt)	**$131 500**	**$164 985**	**$200 579**	$ 238 415	$ 310 135

Year	10	20	30	40
Property $500k @ 6.3%	$ 921091	$1696818	$3125849	$ 5758384
Equity @ 80%	$ 736873	$ 1357455	$ 2500679	$ 4606707
Loan	$ 400000	$ 400000	$ 400000	$ 400000
Borrowing available	$ 336873	$ 957455	$ 2100679	$ 4206707
Property 2 @ $500k	$ 721389	$1328930	$2448132	$ 4509906
Property 2 loan	$ 500000	$ 500000	$ 500000	$ 500000
Property 2 equity	$ 221389	$ 828930	$ 1948132	$ 4009906
Total assets	$1642480	$3025749	$5573981	$10268290
Total debt	$ 900000	$ 900000	$ 900000	$ 900000
Total wealth (assets – debt)	$ 742480	$2125749	$4673981	$ 9368290

Equity for shares vs for property

As discussed, banks are generally comfortable lending against the equity in your property, and you can use the funds borrowed to invest in anything, including more property, shares or any other investment you choose. Your decision can make a big difference to your results.

The big advantage of property is that you will generally be able to borrow more, which can be particularly beneficial in the early stages of your wealth building. For example, if you borrowed $200000 against equity in an existing property, you could use that money as a deposit to purchase another property.

The bank will lend against the equity from your existing property, and then against the equity built up in the new property, allowing you to buy a third investment property with a value around $1 million.

If you were to use the money to invest in shares you wouldn't be able to borrow any further funds, so your total investment would be $200000.

Table 2.3 compares the expected returns on a $200k share portfolio and a $1 million property.

Table 2.3 returns on shares vs property

Year	1	2	3	4
Shares $200k @ 9.8%	$ 220 504	$ 243 112	$ 268 036	$ 295 516
Property $1m @ 6.3%	$ 1 064 852	$ 1 133 908	$ 1 207 444	$ 1 285 748
Property upside	$ 844 348	$ 890 796	$ 939 408	$ 990 232
Year	5	10	20	30
Shares $200k @ 9.8%	$ 325 814	$ 530 774	$ 1 408 608	$ 3 738 266
Property $1m @ 6.3%	$ 1 369 130	$ 1 874 518	$ 3 513 820	$ 6 586 724
Property upside	$ 1 043 316	$ 1 343 744	$ 2 105 212	$ 2 848 458

You can see from this that if your investment is five times as large ($1 million vs $200k), the bigger investment is likely to win over the long term. And in the table above, the total return on property is understated because it takes into account only property growth and not rental income.

This suggests that throughout your Virgin Millionaire journey, you should look to use equity to fund further investments and accelerate your asset building.

But there is a limit to how far you need to push.

Table 2.4 shows how properties of different value will grow over time using the long-term property growth rate of 6.3 per cent.

You can see from this that were you to start with $1 million of investment property value, over 10 years you'd see an investment value increase of $842 182 (after taking away the starting property value). Over 20, 30 and 40 years you'd be looking at growth of $2 393 636, $5 251 697 or $10 516 767.

If you have more property, the growth is even bigger, and faster.

Table 2.4 property investment value over time

Starting value	Year 1	Year 5	Year 10	Year 15
$1 000 000	$1 063 000	$1 357 270	$1 842 182	$ 2 500 339
$2 000 000	$2 126 000	$2 714 540	$3 684 365	$ 5 000 679
$3 000 000	$3 189 000	$4 071 811	$5 526 547	$ 7 501 018
$4 000 000	$4 252 000	$5 429 081	$7 368 730	$10 001 358
$5 000 000	$5 315 000	$6 786 351	$9 210 912	$12 501 697

Starting value	Year 20	Year 30	Year 40
$1 000 000	$ 3 393 636	$ 6 251 697	$11 516 767
$2 000 000	$ 6 787 273	$12 503 394	$23 033 534
$3 000 000	$10 180 909	$18 755 092	$34 550 301
$4 000 000	$13 574 545	$25 006 789	$46 067 068
$5 000 000	$16 968 181	$31 258 486	$57 583 835

This tells me you don't need 10 properties. You probably don't even need five. The more properties you have, the more risk you face. You'll reach a point where you have enough property, and once you get there it doesn't make a lot of sense to keep stretching yourself to buy more.

'Enough' in this context is the amount of property that's needed to put you on track to hit your asset-building and wealth goals, and to make your target level of progress through the Smart Money Stages, in your ideal timeframe.

Once you get to 'enough' property, because you no longer *need* to buy more property you will accumulate equity you could choose to borrow against. It may be worth considering using it to buy shares. In my opinion, borrowing against your property equity to invest in shares isn't really a smart move before this point.

Manage your risk

In this chapter I've covered a lot of the benefits to be gained from using debt to invest. Borrowing to invest is one of my favourite strategies, and I believe it is an important aspect of the journey to real money success.

But you should be aware that borrowing to invest involves risk that needs to be carefully managed. There are four key areas that drive most risk. I will discuss them in some detail so you can cover your bases.

Choosing quality investments

There are two things every investor needs to do to get good returns. First, choose an investment that will increase in value.

When investing in property with borrowed money, you're effectively relying on future growth. It's this growth that will facilitate your next investment, whether it's buying another investment property, investing in shares, or being able to turn off your employment income tap and retire.

If you choose an investment that doesn't grow over the long term, not only will you not make money on it but your equity won't grow. This will reduce your ability to borrow more to invest in the future. And because each property consumes some of your borrowing capacity, a slow-growing property can be a serious spanner in the works of your Virgin Millionaire plan.

Avoiding forced sales

The second thing you need to do to get good results when you invest is to make sure you're never forced to sell your good investment at a bad time.

The aim of any growth investment such as property or shares is to increase in value over time, and if you choose a good investment this is exactly what will happen. But value increases don't happen in a straight line. Ups and downs are to be expected.

Even if you have the best property or share investment, there will be periods when its value will decrease. It may be an effect of what's going on in the economy in Australia and around the world, of market sentiment, of geopolitical factors or of a huge number of other variables.

It's important when you borrow to invest that you have money to fall back on. Your emergency fund needs to be full and you need a buffer for changes to your situation, including your finances, into the future.

If you're forced to sell a good investment at a bad time, you can lose money.

Cashflow risk

The biggest and most complicated area of risk to manage when you borrow to invest is around the cashflow of your debt-funded investment. Any time you borrow, you will need to make regular repayments to cover your debt. These repayments impact your cashflow and savings capacity, and if you can't cover your repayments and all your other expenses you'll be in serious trouble.

You may be forced to make lifestyle sacrifices. In the short term this may be manageable but in the long term it's unsustainable. Either way it's not the pathway I'd recommend for any Virgin Millionaire, and it's unlikely to be the pathway you want for yourself.

Any time you borrow to invest, you need to ensure the investment and associated debt repayments comfortably fit within your means, not only today and next month but into the years ahead. Long-term cashflow is an area most people don't think about as much as they should, yet it carries the most risk.

Starting a family and the costs related to children and schooling, changing jobs or careers, starting a business and relocating to a different suburb or state will have a financial impact on how much money you have to cover debt repayments and investments.

You may buy an ideal property today, but one major change can mean it's no longer a comfortable fit. This will force you to make difficult decisions, such as selling your investment or making other sacrifices.

When setting up your strategy for buying a property take time to consider how possible changed circumstances could impact your income and expenses. Bake this into your planning to ensure you will be able to hold your investment and reap the rewards over the long term.

Interest rate risk

In the first months of 2024, we were looking back on the fastest interest-rate tightening cycle in a generation. Interest rate increases caught most people by surprise.

Many investors in the property market were under so much pressure they needed to sell properties because they simply couldn't keep up their debt repayments. Though they will be able to get back on track, their investing plans have been set back for years.

No one was expecting rates to increase as far or as fast as they did, but it's also fair to say that many didn't plan their borrowing as well as they should have.

Whenever you borrow, you need to be aware that interest rates may increase and plan your investment with this in mind. This is particularly important when rates are below their long-term average, but it's relevant at any time.

How to manage risk effectively when you borrow

The good news is that all these key investment risks can be managed by keeping focused on the same technique: setting up and staying with a rock-solid investment and financial plan. Choose good investments in the first place, then ensure each investment fits well with your money so you get the results you're aiming for.

You won't be forced to sell, the cashflow cost on your investment will fit with the lifestyle you want to live, and you'll be ready and able to cover higher interest costs should it become necessary. This way you'll make a good investment you can comfortably hold for the long term so it can return serious money.

I'll dive deeper into exactly how you can create this plan later, but for now it's enough to know this is a crucial part of investing in general and leveraged investing in particular.

Smart Money Stages and leverage

Debt is an important part of the smart Virgin Millionaire journey, and when combined with good risk management it's one of the most effective ways to accelerate your financial trajectory. But as with any money move, it's important to use debt in line with where you're at with your money.

This links back to the Smart Money Stages outlined in chapter 1, which dictate which moves make sense for you at each stage. Table 2.5 lists the key considerations around leverage and debt at each stage.

Table 2.5 Smart Money Stages: leverage and property

Success outcomes	Foundations	Focus	Optimise	Accelerate	Impact
Property and debt	Understand the importance of property for wealth building.	Own (at least) one quality investment property.	Own more than one quality investment property to support asset/ wealth building.	Own multiple investment properties with deductible debt maximised.	Own your dream home free of non-deductible debt.

Leverage: Foundations

At the Foundations stage, your focus is on setting up the right foundations in each of the key money focus areas. You're setting up the track to run on, and the systems and habits that will drive your future success.

Avoid debt until these foundations are in place. Introducing debt and debt repayments too early is a complication that will make it harder to move to the next stage.

If you're keen to start introducing debt into your investing strategy, the good news is you *can* move through the Foundations stage quickly. This means you won't need to wait long to unleash the power of leverage into your investing strategy.

If you have bad debt, such as interest owing on credit cards or personal loans, be aware this is very different from good investment debt. Bad debt is a handbrake that will hold back your progress, so it needs to be eliminated from your life asap. If you need help, see the free training we've put together at bit.ly/virginmillionaire.

Leverage: Focus

The Focus stage is the first time you'll introduce the power of leverage into your investing as you buy your first investment property, so there will be a big learning curve at this stage around leverage.

I've said it before and I'll no doubt say it again: your first investment property purchase is critical to your progress. You have to get it right. You'll want to get into the property market as soon as possible so you can stop chasing your tail and start benefiting from the rising property market, but it's crucial you invest well to drive the results you want into the future.

That means choosing a quality property that will grow in value, setting the right strategy so you're never forced to sell, preparing for rising interest rates and anticipating things that could change in your future personal circumstances.

When you get it right, you'll benefit from a rock-solid investment that will make you a bunch of money. But you'll also create the lever that will unlock your capacity to invest more in the future without having to touch your own savings.

Leverage: Optimise

You can't reach the Optimise stage without having good debt as part of your investing strategy. By this time you'll have some experience to build on.

At this stage one of your goals will be to acquire your second investment property. It's important you take as much care with this purchase as you did with the first.

Given you already have debt and are considering introducing more, risk management will be a high priority. It's natural to want to rush to take your next investing step, but cutting corners around risk assessment would be a big mistake. Before your second property purchase be sure your emergency fund is a sufficient buffer against the unexpected. Also, have good income protection insurance in place to protect your investments and your progress.

By applying the same careful planning approach to your second property purchase, you'll benefit from picking up another quality investment that will make you money. But the other benefits are arguably even more important.

You'll now have two solid property investments growing your equity and your future borrowing capacity, and creating some helpful tax deductions on top.

Planning is more complicated at the Optimise stage because more is going on with your money. If you haven't already found a good financial adviser you should do so before planning your second investment property purchase.

Leverage: Accelerate

At the Accelerate stage you'll either have reached, or be close to reaching, the ideal level of leverage you need to take you all the way to smart money freedom. Your property equity should be compounding at a solid rate each year and the bank will be happy to lend you more money than you actually want to borrow.

That said, as you focus on setting up your money to provide your ideal lifestyle level of spending, you may still look at leverage as an accelerator to lift your financial trajectory. Using equity to invest in shares can be considered at this point if it isn't needed for further property investing.

With higher debt levels, and with true money success just around the corner, risk management should remain a critical focus. The good news is that by this stage it should be easier for you to manage risk when borrowing to invest, because you have more money and investments behind you.

Once again, the complexity of your planning will go up another level at this stage, and in my (admittedly biased) opinion it's borderline reckless to try managing all this on your own. Look at bringing in professional financial support. With the money you now have behind you, the upside of good advice will more than cover the cost.

You're now close to the Impact stage, where you'll most likely be looking to purchase your dream home. This shouldn't be your main focus, but it should be part of your planning. Buying your own home without the benefit of a non-deductible mortgage is your goal at the next stage, so you'll want to ensure your debt strategy is consistent with your plan.

Leverage: Impact

At the Impact stage you'll be in a position to borrow more money than you want to. Given you're getting close to smart money freedom, you may not *need* to borrow more, but you also don't want to leave money on the table.

With the money you have behind you, you'll be able to position yourself to manage risk comfortably within your strategy and increase borrowing to further amplify your wealth building.

Buying your dream home becomes possible without compromising your progress towards smart money freedom. The key here is to become free of non-tax-deductible debt as quickly as possible.

Owning your own home without a mortgage means that by definition you're going to have a huge amount of equity that you *could* use to invest, if this makes sense. You'll want to be smart with your planning around this to ensure you're using your money to its fullest potential.

At this point you will have a fully functioning money dream team (I'll cover this later) so you'll be able to use them to drive results around your leverage and what it allows you to do with your investing.

THE WRAP

Debt can be scary, and it's sensible to be concerned about facing risk. But much of the risk associated with borrowing to invest can be managed if you plan smartly.

The benefits of using debt to invest are compelling: more returns faster plus tax breaks on top. Debt isn't for everyone, but for most people, so long as it's used wisely, it's one of the most effective ways to accelerate their progress.

The first step in your debt-funded investment journey is likely to be property. While purchasing your first property isn't easy, it can be straightforward if

(continued)

you understand the process. Once you've taken that first big step your equity, and your money momentum, start to build. And this makes the next steps easier.

Risk management is all important with any investment, but when you're borrowing to invest this risk is amplified, so smart planning and good management are important.

When you get it right, it's like pouring rocket fuel on your wealth building. You make more progress in less time, ticking off your money milestones and creating a future that wouldn't have been possible from saving and investing alone.

Take action

- Assess where you currently sit in the debt and property financial focus area.

- If you have bad debt, get rid of it asap. This free training will help: https://bit.ly/virginmillionaire.

- Get clear on the big difference between tax-deductible investment debt and other debt.

- Start the process of finding a compatible mortgage broker.

- Assess your borrowing capacity today to understand your starting point.

- Run the numbers on buying a home vs an investment property as a thought exercise to determine the true difference between these options.

- Understand the three key risks that come with debt-funded investing and how you can manage and reduce them.

CHAPTER 3

Not all property wisdom is wise

Property investment is one of the fastest and most effective ways to build wealth, but this area is filled by myths and misconceptions. Much of the commonly accepted wisdom is just plain wrong.

As discussed in the previous chapter, the driver that makes property the most effective investment to build wealth is leverage. Hardly anyone buys property with cash. Most property purchases are funded with debt, which means you can purchase a much more valuable asset than you could fund using just the money you've saved. This leverage accelerates your investment and wealth building, and when you get it right it will deliver better results than any other investment.

But properties in Australia are expensive. They come with a high price tag, large buy and sell costs and significant tax implications. And there are some real risks that need to be managed. Mistakes can be costly and slow your progress, resulting in years, even decades, of lost time.

In this chapter I debunk some common property myths and help you avoid mistakes and pitfalls so you can set up a winning property that will help you get ahead the smart way.

The sooner you buy your first home, the poorer you'll be

Most people find this idea a little jarring, but this isn't just my opinion. It's based in simple maths.

Let me explain.

Under the investing and tax rules in Australia, you receive no tax breaks for buying a home. You save your deposit from your pay after tax. You pay your purchase costs with after-tax dollars. You make your mortgage payments with after-tax income. And you fund all your ongoing property costs with, you guessed it, after-tax dollars.

If instead you were to buy the same property as an investment, things would be different. Because the government wants people to invest successfully and rely less on government benefits in the future, they incentivise investment through tax breaks.

When you buy an investment property, all your ongoing costs are tax deductible. Your mortgage interest costs, the cost of maintenance and repairs, your council or strata rates and any other costs relating to the property are fully tax deductible.

When you claim these costs as a tax deduction, you don't get the full amount back, but you do receive a refund at whatever your marginal tax rate is. If your income is above $45 000, your tax rate will be at least 32 per cent, and could be up to 47 per cent if you're on the top marginal tax rate.

This means you'll receive a refund for property investment expenses of at least 32 per cent, almost a third of all property expenses, and it could be as high as almost half of every dollar you pay.

This makes a big difference to how quickly you get ahead. Let me explain using some numbers.

How much does it cost to own an investment property?

The average cost of owning an investment property worth $1 million is $33356 p.a.

You might wonder why on earth anyone would bother buying an investment property if it's going to cost almost $30k every year. It's a fair question, but the income and costs of an investment property are only one half of the picture. The other is the growth in the value of the property over time.

In Australia the long-term annual growth rate of the average property is 6.3 per cent. This means the annual growth on a $1 million investment property should average out at around $63k.

The numbers stack up nicely here. If you're paying $33k for a $63k benefit, you're ahead by ~$29k every single year. Of course, these figures are based on some assumptions, and the past doesn't necessarily predict the future, but there is still plenty of room for you to come out way ahead.

Initial costs of buying a property

When you purchase a property you need to pay some initial costs such as stamp duty, building and pest inspections, and legal costs. These on average equate to around 5 per cent of the property value, which on a $1 million property means $50000 in initial purchase costs.

Ongoing costs of owning a property

These costs include things like strata fees for apartments and townhouses or council rates for houses, water rates, insurance costs, property management fees, repairs and maintenance.

These costs tend to average out at around 1 per cent of the property value, so for a $1 million property this equates to $10000 each year in ongoing costs.

Then there's mortgage interest. According to Finder.com, in March 2024 the average variable mortgage interest rate in Australia was 7.24 per cent. Based on a 30-year mortgage of $1 050 000 (purchase price + costs), your annual interest is $76 020.

Current interest rates are significantly higher than long-term averages, so the numbers we cover here are close to a worst-case scenario.

In the example that follows I've used the average interest rate, but I've noted that by shopping around you should be able to achieve a much lower rate. The sharpest variable mortgage interest rates at the time of writing are sitting at 5.69 per cent, significantly lower than the average rate.

For this example I want to be clear that borrowing the full property purchase price as well as your costs is only possible if you're either using equity from another property or a family guarantee loan. The reason the entire amount has been included in this example is to show you the full costs of the entire purchase.

If you purchase a property with a cash deposit, your loan will be smaller and your mortgage repayments will be lower than the figures in this example.

Property costs are tax deductible

I will cover this in detail when discussing tax, but the short version is that when you borrow money to invest, all costs related to that investment are tax deductible against your other income.

Based on Australian marginal tax rates, if your taxable income is above $45 000, your marginal tax rate + Medicare levy is 32 per cent. This means that for every dollar your investment property costs you, you'll receive a tax refund of $0.32. If your income and tax rate are higher, you'll get even more back at tax time.

This helps to reduce the after-tax cost of running your property as it essentially gives you at least a third of whatever you pay back at tax time.

Financial benefits of an investment property

When you own an investment property the benefits are twofold. The rent paid by your tenants is income, and the property will increase in value over time.

According to CoreLogic, the average gross rental income on property in Australian capital cities as at September 2023 was 3.71 per cent and, as outlined above, the long-term growth rate on property is 6.3 per cent.

Bringing it together

Purchase costs:

- Property value: $1 000 000
- Purchase costs @ 5 per cent: $50 000
- Total funds needed: $1 050 000.

Ongoing income:

- Gross (headline) rental income @ 3.71 per cent: $37 100 p.a.

Ongoing expenses:

- Ongoing property expenses @ 1 per cent: –$10 000
- Mortgage interest: –$76 020
- Total costs: –$86 020
- Cashflow cost/net income: –$48 920
- Tax refund at 32 per cent: +$15 564
- Net holding costs after tax: $33 356.

Property growth:

- Average annual growth @ 6.3 per cent: $63 000.

Note that this assumes your income is only above $45k with the associated tax rate. If your income is higher the tax benefits will be even greater.

(continued)

But where do you live?

It's a fair question. To relate directly to this example, let's say you rent an identical property (the house next door) with exactly the same value. You spend the same amount on rent as you receive in rental income on your investment property. In this case, your property related costs + growth would be as follows:

- Net cost of your property: $33 356
- Money spent on rent (identical property): $37 100
- Total cost of $1 million investment property + $1 million rental (to live in): $70 456.

I'll come back to these numbers.

How does buying your own home compare?

At the start of this chapter I made the bold claim that buying your home will make you poor. Let me show you exactly what I meant. Here I've included an example that uses the same numbers as before, but with one big difference. You can no longer claim the costs as a tax deduction.

Purchase costs:

- Property value: $1 000 000
- Purchase costs @ 5%: $50 000
- Total funds needed: $1 050 000.

Ongoing income:

- Rental income: none because you live in the property.

Ongoing expenses:

- Ongoing property expenses @ 1%: –$10 000
- Mortgage interest: –$76 020
- Total costs: –$86 020
- Cashflow cost/net income: –$86 020
- Tax refund: none
- Net holding costs after tax: $86 020.

Property growth:

- Average annual growth @ 6.3%: $63 000.

Net result:

Based on owning this property as your home, these are the cashflow costs:

- Net income (cost) of your property: $86 020
- Money spent on rent: $0
- Total cashflow cost: $86 020.

If you own a property and live in it yourself, the total cost to you each year will be $86 020. If you were to hold the same property as an investment, the costs would be $70 456, reflecting a difference of $15 564 p.a.

In other words, you own the property, and it achieves the same growth every year into the future. Meanwhile you live in an identical property, same value, space and comfort levels.

But if you choose to buy your property as an investment, you're going to be more than $15k better off every single year. That's over $15k you can use to save, invest or use to pay down debt each year. This money can build your savings and investments, and ultimately help you achieve smart money freedom.

Owning your home comes with a clear cost in excess of what you need to pay to buy a property as an investment. The conventional wisdom says rent is dead money so you should buy your first home as soon as possible. It says that owning your own home means security.

The conventional wisdom is wrong.

For some people, buying their own home is really important. For whatever deep-seated personal or emotional reasons, it's a big deal.

If that's you, then pushing to buy your own home is totally okay. But it's important you recognise there's a cost. You will have less money for saving and investing in the years ahead.

If you can cover this extra cost and still make the progress you really want through investing, all power to you. But keep in mind that affording your own home doesn't just mean being able to cover your mortgage repayments.

As a Virgin Millionaire, being able to afford your own home means you can not only cover your mortgage repayments but also pay off your mortgage completely in a timeframe you've chosen, and have enough left over to build your investments at a rate you're happy with.

If you can't do these three things at the time you purchase your own home, you'll have to compromise on investment success and security, and this will compromise your ability to progress towards smart money freedom.

Right now property affordability is at an all-time low. So many people I talk to feel getting ahead financially is hard, and they're right. But know that rentvesting is a path every single person can either follow now or position themselves for in the future, and it's one that will give you more money with which to make more progress in less time.

When you're at the Foundations and Focus stages, by definition you're not (yet) on track to hit your version of smart money freedom in a timeframe you're happy with. Buying your own home will slow down your financial progress even further, so in my opinion buying your own home while at either of these stages is a bad financial decision.

Early in the Optimise stage, you're on track to achieve smart money freedom in your desired timeframe. If you buy a home at this stage, however, it will also slow down your progress towards your goal, so I suggest buying your own home is possible but probably not ideal.

When you enter the Accelerate stage, you'll be exceeding your financial targets in your chosen timeframe. If buying your own home is important to you, start planning around this.

At the Impact stage, you've achieved smart money freedom and, if you haven't done so already, you should be thinking about making your dream-home purchase. You can now do this with total peace of mind, knowing that all the other elements of your money strategy are still going to work, and work well.

First-home buyer initiatives

A number of schemes are available to help first-home buyers get into the property market. The government knows that housing affordability is an issue, and they want to help people get onto the property ladder.

Most of these schemes require you to be buying a property as your own home, as opposed to an investment property, so you may be wondering how this relates to buying your first property as an investment.

The way I see it, you can aim to buy a property as an investment, with the sole focus on choosing a good property that will make you good money into the future and support your Virgin Millionaire journey. If you can do this, AND take advantage of schemes to get the same property faster by spending less money, then this is something you should consider.

Most first-home buyer benefits only require you to live in the property for a short time before you can move out and run it as an investment and benefit from all the advantages outlined in this chapter.

(continued)

> If you can't buy a high-quality property that will be a solid long-term investment AND access the government benefits, in my opinion, and based on the numbers, you're going to be way better off in the years ahead if you give up the first-home buyer benefits rather than compromising on the quality of your investment. It may take slightly longer to buy your property, but you'll likely end up hundreds of thousands of dollars better off over the years ahead.
>
> A good adviser or mortgage broker will be a big help here with running the numbers and planning your purchase.

When to buy your own home

Owning your dream home is an important part of true money success, and it's achievable if you're prepared to put in the work to make it happen. That said, it's important your home purchase aligns with your financial position. The amount you spend on your dream home must be consistent with your financial trajectory.

I've seen too many people fall into the conventional-wisdom trap, buy their own home too early in their money journey and pay a heavy price. If you do this, you may suffer for it for years, often decades. Your investment progress will be slowed. You'll be frustrated because you can't move ahead at the rate you want, and you'll be stressed by the significant gap between where you are and where you want to be. I get that buying your own home is a nice thing to do; I just don't think it's worth the price tag.

Buying your dream home at the wrong time in your journey will seriously compromise your financial progress. Timing is everything, and number-crunching will be crucial. If the numbers don't stack up, now isn't the right time to buy your home.

But all is not lost. It's an opportunity for you to focus on building your investments and wealth. You'll make faster progress because a big chunk of your savings isn't needed to pay a mortgage with after-tax income. With every month and year your investments and wealth continue to build, buying your own home in a way that's consistent with your Virgin Millionaire goals becomes more achievable.

Balance your home and non-home assets

Tony and Ava were a young couple in their early thirties who had done incredibly well for themselves. They had both started their careers working for a startup tech company that had grown exponentially and listed on the stock exchange.

They were both granted some shares in the early days when the company was relatively small and the share price very low. The shares increased in value and they finally cashed out around $4 million, which essentially set up their future.

You might think this would mean they could do whatever they wanted.

These guys were pretty switched on. Good at saving, not crazy spenders. When they came to us they already understood the power of index-fund investing and had used it to make a bunch of money.

What Tony and Ava really wanted was to buy their own home close to the beach in Sydney's Eastern Suburbs, a house big enough for them and their kids.

But when we ran the numbers, things just weren't adding up. They had enough to buy the home they wanted but to do it would tie up almost all their money, leaving relatively little for investing.

Tony and Ava were planning to have their second child. They wanted Ava to be able to take a year's maternity leave then work part-time for a while.

Tony had left the tech company that had delivered their big payday and wanted the flexibility to work only with companies he truly believed in.

And with a growing family, he didn't want a high-pressure role that would prevent him from being the dad he wanted to be. That meant lower salary expectations for at least the next five years.

When we put all these variables together, we could see Tony and Ava wouldn't have much savings capacity, at least until their kids started school. Putting all their money into their own home would prevent them from rebuilding their investments.

Tony and Ava realised they couldn't actually afford their home *and* hit their other money targets. When it came to the long-term impact, the cost was just too great.

The good news is that Tony and Ava had a great foundation on which to build. They would reach the stage where their dream-home purchase was possible and they could still make smart investing moves. It was just that this time wasn't now.

They ended up buying two quality investment properties at the same time as they built a substantial exchange-traded funds portfolio. Their solid foothold in the property market meant that even if prices continued to rise, they could use the investment properties to fund their home purchase. And the tax deductions, along with the cost of funding investment properties rather than their own home, meant there was a lot more money available every year for further investment. Their lifestyle remained flexible while they looked forward to a more comfortable future home purchase.

Of course, your smart money freedom number excludes the value of your home, as smart money freedom means having enough return on investments to fund your ideal lifestyle. This gives a more accurate picture of your investment wealth position because, while your home does have a value, as long as you're living in it, it won't generate income.

However, your home mortgage is included as a debt against your smart money freedom number because until you clear that debt you will need to make repayments.

The more you spend on your own home, the longer it's going to take you to achieve smart money freedom. For example, if you're targeting annual ideal lifestyle spending of $200k, your smart money freedom number is going to be $4 million. This is how much you need in net investments (investments less debt) outside your home.

If your dream home is a $1 million property, to hit smart money freedom you'll need to build and grow your total asset position, less debt, to $5 million. If you spend $3 million on your dream home, you'll need to build $7 million to hit smart money freedom—clearly a much bigger undertaking.

This isn't to say that you shouldn't spend what you want to on your dream home. The entire premise of being a Virgin Millionaire is that you're setting up your ideal lifestyle, which means you'll be able to live in your dream home while living and spending the way you want.

It simply means the balance you strike between your home and non-home assets will be a critical driver of how quickly you'll reach your version of smart money freedom.

For now, I just want to plant the seed in your mind that buying your own home is a costly exercise, and the more you spend the more work you're going to have to do in order to save and invest. We'll dive into this in chapter 9, when I cover how to map out and plan your smart money freedom journey.

How to choose a good property

We've now covered whether you should buy your own home or an investment property and how much to spend. You're getting a good sense of your next property move and how you can use property to accelerate your Virgin Millionaire journey.

Remember, if you're buying property to build your investments and wealth, the one crucial outcome is that your property increases in value over time.

This increase will be captured if you choose to sell your property and use the funds for other types of investments — or to buy your dream home or cover your ideal lifestyle spending. And as your property increases in value, you can borrow against the increase to invest further in more property, shares or other investments.

Because property is expensive to buy and sell, because selling property has tax implications and because property involves a lot of work from a money admin perspective, you'll benefit from avoiding buying and selling properties as much as possible.

Your aim will be to find a good property you can buy today knowing that, because it will continue to grow in value into the future, you will never need to sell it.

So, what makes a good property and how do you find one?

There are heaps of different opinions and ideas around this, and the online advice can be overwhelming. Most property gurus are adamant theirs is the only way.

I'd argue there are many ways to be right when it comes to property.

You can chase property hotspots, you can buy-renovate-flip, you can buy off the plan and sell before completion for a profit. You can build a positively geared property portfolio, you can target distressed properties, or you can follow a simple buy-and-hold strategy.

All these strategies can work.

While I won't insist mine is the only way, I'll unpack my personal strategy and explain why it works for me and why I recommend it to the people I help with their money.

The short version is this:

- Buy a premium property.
- Target as much land as possible.
- Target low ongoing property costs.
- Hold for the long term.

The result is you'll own a good investment property you can hold long term with strong rental and low vacancy rates. You'll have fewer properties and fewer headaches. This approach goes a long way to ensuring you'll get growth and make money.

Buying and holding for the long term involves a lot less work than buying and selling regularly. And you don't need to agonise over the right time to buy or sell. The right time is dictated by your strategy as opposed to what's going on in the market.

This approach is simple and low risk and historically it has been much more effective than most other property-buying strategies. It's not exciting—some might even call it boring—but in my experience, simple is effective and boring is profitable.

Premium properties

I'll illustrate this discussion with the example of the Sydney property market because it's the market I know best.

In Sydney the upper end of our target price range for an investment property is around $1.8 million. The reason there's a top end is because once you get much over this price point, rental income starts to reduce relative to property value (rental yield), which makes your investment more expensive to hold.

At this price point you can buy a two-bedroom apartment in Bondi Beach, Surry Hills or Mosman. It may even include a car space. Putting aside for a minute the silliness of this relative to other property markets around Australia—and the world—let's look at the dynamics of such an investment.

The two fundamental drivers of the value of your investment over time are supply and demand. Supply of properties like these is limited and demand is strong.

All suburbs within five kilometres of the Sydney CBD are fully built out and in most of them council zoning restricts large new developments. At the same time, they are experiencing strong population growth and more is projected into the future, so demand will remain high. Low rental vacancy rates will protect your income.

When you're choosing suburbs, I suggest sticking to those that have lower density levels with fewer apartments and more houses. Over time all suburbs will eventually increase their density levels. New developments are almost always higher density than existing properties. You can benefit from density increases in the suburb. If you own a house in an area where more units are being built, the value of your property will increase over time for two reasons: first, it will be more desirable to some to live in a house rather than a unit; and second, your property will have more development potential.

Suburbs like Green Square and Ultimo, which contain a lot of big apartment buildings, are slightly less desirable in investment terms than areas like Mosman, Glebe and Double Bay, where strict zoning restrictions ensure very few new apartments will be built. Lower supply and growing demand ensure stronger growth.

Because rents aren't cheap, your tenants are likely to be professionals working in or around the CBD in jobs that pay well. Rental income is likely to be more stable, too, since your tenants are less likely to lose income and be unable to afford their rent.

The resale market will also be strong, with potential buyers ranging from first- or second-home buyers to downsizers to investors. Because the value will hold up well, should you want to exit, the property should sell quickly.

Target as much land as possible

A property's value is not in bricks and mortar. Reserve Bank of Australia data show the value of land to be roughly double that of the value of what is built on it: around two-thirds of the total value is in the land, and only one-third is in the building. Historically, the value of land holds and appreciates but the value of a building declines with age.

So the more land you own, the more the value of your property will increase.

How much land you're likely to be looking at when you buy a dwelling will depend on whether it is a:

1. freestanding house
2. townhouse or terrace
3. unit or apartment.

This ranking should be your guide because it reflects which types of property have performed best historically. According to CoreLogic data, Australian house values have increased 453 per cent over the past 30 years, compared to 307 per cent for units.

If buying a freestanding house is not yet possible for you, just work your way down the list until you find something that will be a good investment and work with your investment plan.

If you're considering a unit, keep in mind that the ratio of land to each unit varies. If you own an apartment in a block of six, you own one sixth of the land. If you are in a block of 60 apartments, you own one sixtieth, and if you are in a block of 600, you'll own one six hundredth of the land. The bigger the block, the less land you own; the less land you own, the less growth you'll typically see over time.

Aim for lower ongoing costs

Whether you buy a house or an apartment, keeping costs low will make it easier for you to carry the investment.

If you buy more than one investment property (as you should), each one will use up some of your cashflow. The more you spend on ongoing property expenses, the more you're going to have to put in out of your own pocket.

Property features like pools, gyms and elevators are nice to have but expensive to operate and maintain. From a pure investment perspective, if you can avoid costly features you'll minimise your costs and have more money available for your next investment.

Hold for the long term

Property is expensive to buy and sell, and these costs will eat into your profits. If you buy quality properties from the start with a good strategy behind you, it's likely you'll sell one good property in order to buy another, incurring both sale and purchase costs as well as, potentially, capital gains tax. When you run the numbers, this is unlikely to make much sense.

In the wealth-building phase of your Virgin Millionaire journey, I strongly advocate buying properties to hold for the long term.

Three property mistakes to avoid

Making a property investing mistake can be extremely costly in both the short and the long term. I'll unpack the top three property mistakes I see people make so you can avoid them.

Don't sacrifice growth for income

There is a lot of talk out there about building a positively geared portfolio, but it can lead to serious issues with your investing.

Don't get me wrong. Buying positive-income properties is good. But it's a mistake to compromise on the growth potential of a property to get a higher rental income return. This is because properties with a higher rental yield typically have lower growth prospects—not always, but most of the time. For example, properties in regional and remote areas will deliver you a higher rental income yield, but they usually don't grow in value at the rate property in a capital city does.

If you can find a property that has strong growth potential and meets the criteria I've outlined here, and it has a strong rental income yield, great. But, in my view, it's a mistake to compromise on the growth of your property for a few extra bucks in rent.

Investing for tax purposes alone

An investment property comes with some tax perks. Negative gearing allows you to deduct your mortgage interest and ongoing property costs from your income. And if you buy a new property, the tax deductions get even bigger through the magic of depreciation.

Depreciation is the reduction in the value of the fittings and fixtures of a property over time. When you buy a new home, before you move in everything is brand new and worth the full retail replacement value.

Say you buy an oven worth $2500. If you try to sell it once you've cooked up your first pasta bake, it's used and you might get only $2000 for it. Once you've cooked 100 pasta bakes over a few years, you might be able to get only $1000. This reduction in value with use and time is called depreciation.

Depreciation doesn't really cost you money. It's not as though you pay money out of your pocket as things in your property come to be worth less. But with the tax rules, you can claim this depreciation in value as a tax-deductible expense and you receive money back at tax time. Depreciation is typically strong over the first seven years after a property is completed, and reduces to close to zero beyond this point when the property is considered to have been fully depreciated.

Depreciation can transform what would be a negatively geared property that costs you money each month into a positive cashflow investment after the tax benefits are factored in.

But it's easy to be blinded by tax benefits and compromise your investment. If you fall into this trap, you might get some great tax deductions for a limited time, but find yourself in a difficult situation once the benefits end and you are faced with the reality of a poor investment.

You may need to sell your property at a small gain, or even a loss, but more importantly you'll have missed out on purchasing a property that makes you good money in line with average long-term growth rates.

I'll let you in on a little secret. If a property (or any other investment for that matter) isn't a good investment without the tax benefits, it was never a good investment to begin with. Tax benefits should only ever be the cream on top, not the reason to invest.

Buying off the plan

This one is a little controversial, and for good reason. Many investors have made a lot of money from buying property off the plan, but there's one big downside I can't get past.

Buying property off the plan means purchasing a property before it's built, typically through a developer. You agree on the price you'll pay for the property and sign your purchase contract before the property is finished. Once the property is completed, the purchase is finalised and the property is yours.

The advantage of buying a property off the plan, particularly in a rising property market, is that you lock in the price of the property today, and by the time the contract is completed, the property could be worth more.

But if the market falls or if your property was overpriced or if mortgage rules change, you can run into serious trouble. There's also the risk of your developer going bust in the middle of your build and leaving you stuck. The long-term impacts can seriously affect your plan to replace your salary by investing.

I worked with a client in 2018 who had purchased a property off the plan. She bought a good, well-priced house in the Hunter Valley region in NSW. The completion date was mid 2019. Her income was stable and increasing over time. Things were looking good, but this property purchase turned into one of the most stressful experiences I've been involved with.

The problem came because of the Banking Royal Commission (2017–2019). The banks got in a lot of trouble for not being robust enough in their assessment of people's borrowing abilities, and as a result the Australian Prudential Regulation Authority (APRA) mandated set rules for how much an individual could borrow.

Unfortunately for my client, the assessment meant that even though her income was increasing, under the new regulations her borrowing power reduced significantly. This meant that as it came time to complete the purchase, she had to scramble so she didn't lose the $100k+ deposit she'd put down.

This is an extreme example, but it shows how buying off the plan can be seriously stressful and potentially expensive.

Since this time the rapid interest-rate-tightening cycle and the dip in the property market in 2022 and 2023 have impacted a lot of off-the-plan property purchases. There have been countless stories of people who ran their property affordability and borrowing capacity numbers based on interest rates that were much lower than those they could access when it came time to complete their purchase. For these people, affordability was a challenge, and a number of them have been unable to complete their property purchase, losing money and time.

Because the potential downsides of buying off the plan outweigh the potential upsides, in my opinion this strategy should be avoided.

Smart Money Stages and property

When it comes to investing in property the smart moves again depend on the stage you're at. Table 3.1 outlines the key considerations at each Smart Money Stage for property. Remember though that, given leverage and property are so closely linked, you might benefit from reviewing the guide in chapter 2 on leverage.

Table 3.1 Smart Money Stages and property

Success outcomes	Foundations	Focus	Optimise	Accelerate	Impact
Property and debt	Understand the importance of property for wealth building.	Own (at least) one quality investment property.	Own more than one quality investment property to support asset/wealth-building.	Own multiple investment properties with deductible debt maximised.	Own your dream home free of non-deductible debt.

Property: Foundations

At the Foundations stage you probably won't have property in your strategy, but it's important you're aware of how property works and how to build a winning property strategy. You should also recognise the difference between buying your own home compared to buying property as an investment, and why it's crucial you get the timing of each of these moves right.

Building this knowledge at the Foundations stage and before you actually buy a property will help you avoid a lot of the noise that surrounds property. And when you are ready to buy you will be set up for greater success sooner.

Property: Focus

At the Focus stage it's game on. This is the time to let the knowledge, skills and approach you've built at the Foundations stage shine. It's worth repeating that your first property purchase may be the single most important money move you'll ever make, so give it the respect and attention it deserves.

Plan smart with your numbers, choose a good property with strong supply and demand fundamentals, and consider getting some professional advice before you buy. Ideally you should do your property planning (at least) 12 months before your purchase.

This timing may seem excessive, but it's worth getting your strategy right before you start searching. It will save you a heap of time, but more importantly it will reduce the risk of your emotions influencing an investment decision that should be calculated and numbers based.

Property: Optimise

At the Optimise stage you'll buy your second investment property. More property will result in the growth that will push you through the Smart Money Stage into the levels beyond. You have to get it right.

For your second property purchase you'll probably choose a higher-value property to drive more asset growth, which means your planning will need to be even more careful than it was for your first purchase.

It will be difficult to do this on your own, so if you haven't already done so this may be the time to engage professionals to help you with strategy.

Because you now have more money behind you, you may be tempted to buy your own home at this stage. It's important to tread carefully here and only buy your own home if it fits with the other things going on with your money. You've worked hard to reach this position, so you don't want to undo all your hard work and back yourself into a corner.

Property: Accelerate

At the Accelerate stage, depending on what's going on with your money, you may or may not decide to acquire more property. If you do, you'll use the same strategies to choose a quality investment asset as you did at the Foundations and Focus stages.

It may become possible to buy your own home without sabotaging your investing and wealth building. If buying your own home is important to you and if the numbers work, then you can make this happen. But the numbers are the critical ingredient. Don't compromise and risk stuffing it up when you're so close to getting to the Impact stage.

Property: Impact

At the Impact stage more possibilities for property open up. You should be looking to buy your dream home, with a clear plan for being debt free. This is an exciting time, but it needs planning.

As I've outlined, the balance between your home and non-home investments is the truest measure of your real wealth levels, so finding the ideal balance is mission critical. While this is a complicated and highly important decision, you have all the tools you need to make it happen in a way that will work for you.

By this stage you know how to plan in a smart way so your risk is managed and you're thinking beyond the short term. Apply this approach to your home purchase and you'll benefit by getting the right roof over your head, at the same time ensuring it will deliver the investment upside you want. Leverage your money dream team here for optimal results.

THE WRAP

Property is an important element of your money success, and getting your approach right from the start will deliver serious benefits. You'll get onto the property ladder sooner and choose better property investments that will deliver better returns, all with less stress and effort.

There's a big difference between buying your own home and buying an investment property, and you need to be clear on the value of your home compared to your non-home investments.

Make the right move at the right time, and the result will be more savings and investing capacity for longer and more confidence and peace of mind when you decide it's the right time to buy your own home. Much of the conventional wisdom that surrounds buying a home is wrong, and being influenced by it can be seriously costly.

If you don't already own property, plan out your first purchase in granular detail asap (read now) so you have a clear path to your target. Don't feel you are on your own. Professional advice will pay for itself many times over as you progress more quickly towards your target and your investments grow more once you get there.

Finding a good property that will deliver for you now and into the future is critical to the success of your Virgin Millionaire journey. Know there are a lot of ways to be right with property, but some ways are more consistently effective than others. Choose wisely and you'll be rewarded.

Avoiding property mistakes is the final element of becoming a true property pro, and there are some painful ones to avoid.

Australians love property—owning it, buying it and talking about it. But all the noise can be confusing and overwhelming. In some cases, it can push you to make costly mistakes that can hold back your progress.

Property can be complicated, but it doesn't need to be. If you take the right approach and get your focus right, you'll be set to get the results you want without headaches, stress or missteps.

Take action

- Recognise the power of property investing to accelerate your investing and wealth building.

- Review the section on own home vs investment property until you're crystal clear on why the conventional wisdom on home ownership is wrong.

- Learn about the first-home buyer benefits that apply in your state and how these can help you get onto the property ladder.

- Engage a mortgage broker and/or a financial adviser to help you build your property strategy.

- Make a mental note for your planning about the importance of balancing the proportion of your assets that is tied up in your home and the proportion that is in income-generating investments.

- Understand how to choose a good property any time you choose to invest in real estate.

- Set the property philosophy you want to follow when you invest in property.

- Understand the three main property-buying risks and how to avoid them.

- Set a clear timeline for buying your next property.

CHAPTER 4

Replace your salary by investing

Investing is the simplest way to guarantee you will become a Virgin Millionaire. The equation is simple:

$$\text{Good investments} \times \text{money in} \times \text{time} = \text{results}$$

The variables are how much money you put in and for how long, but the results are the same. It's not a question of whether you'll get there, it's a question of when.

But you have to invest.

As discussed in chapter 1, saving money in cash means your money is going backwards. Because cash savings won't get you to smart money freedom, investing is a crucial part of your future.

But if you haven't got much (or any) experience in investing, it can seem complicated and confusing, and it's easy to get stuck on the starting line. There seem to be so many options, so many methods out there, to say nothing of mixed messages. This all leads to fear of getting it wrong, and that can be paralysing.

The good news is that when you understand investing and how it can go wrong, things become simple. I'll begin by unpacking some common investing traps so you can avoid them and then I'll cover how you can invest smarter to accelerate your progress through the Smart Money Stages, replace your salary by investing and make faster progress towards becoming a Virgin Millionaire.

Listening to the gurus

When you search the internet, you'll be bombarded by the 157 000 best ways to invest. Thousands of people and companies that claim to have cracked the investing code will promise you fast results with very little risk.

This is all total BS.

It's easy to fall into the trap of listening to this noise because we really want the results these gurus promise. The difficulty goes up another level when they showcase carefully selected wins from their investing history as evidence their approach works.

Imagine I introduce you to someone who has correctly picked the outcome of a coin toss 100 times in row. You might think that person either is psychic or has some special skill that allows them to figure out the result before it happens.

The reality is that while the outcome of a coin toss is entirely random, it can be engineered. If you have enough people guessing the outcome of a coin toss, there's a 50/50 probability someone will guess correctly.

If only one person is guessing, they'll strike out pretty quickly. But if 10, 100, 1000 or more people are guessing the outcome, probability dictates someone will guess correctly a phenomenal number of times.

And when it comes to investing, there are hundreds of millions of investors around the world. They're all choosing different investments and doing different things, but probability dictates some amazing success stories. These may appear to be the effect of secret knowledge but in fact such successes are random.

Warren Buffett, who is widely accepted as one of the world's best investors of the past half century or so, made a now-famous bet. He wanted to prove the world's best investors couldn't perform as well as an index fund investment, so he threw out the challenge to the biggest and best investors in the world. He was so confident he put $1 million on the line as a wager.

Don't worry if you're not across index funds yet. All you need to know for now is that it tracks the entire share market and instead of picking individual stocks, invests a small amount in literally every single company listed.

In terms of this bet, the index fund was up against a hedge fund, which pools investor money and is run by an investment manager or a team of investment managers. Their mandate is to make as much money as possible.

These funds typically work with a heap of weird and complex investments and instruments that I'll unpack in chapter 5.

Hedge funds invest in everything from precious metals like gold and silver and the traditional share market, but they also buy debt finance and bonds, invest in currencies and foreign exchange, and buy up office buildings and infrastructure projects like toll roads. And they use complex financial instruments such as options, warrants and short selling to further drive investment returns.

In this bet, Buffett went to the biggest hedge funds in the world and bet that their best managers, with virtually unlimited resources and experience behind them, wouldn't do as well over a 10-year period as a basic index fund that blindly tracks the share market without using any smarts or tricky investing strategies.

Buffett won the bet with flying colours only seven years into the period of the bet.

Investing can be complicated but it doesn't have to be.

Small vs big company risk

One myth that catches out many first-time investors is that not all risk is created equal.

When it comes to the performance of a small company, it can be difficult to predict the years in which it will see strong growth and those in which it won't. But the bigger the company, the more predictable the growth.

This predictability comes from the fact that the bigger a company becomes, the more experience it has in its field of operations. It builds a track record, a customer base and operational capabilities, all of which create financial stability. The implication is that its returns will be more stable, less volatile, than those of a smaller company.

For the world's largest companies, the level of stability goes up a notch. The biggest companies are leaders in their field. They have significant brand loyalty and value and a proven track record over a number of years—often decades or even centuries.

The implication for investors is that if you were to invest in one or a number of small companies, your returns are likely to vary significantly from year to year. If you invest in the largest companies, your investment returns will be more stable, consistent and predictable.

It's worth noting that the bigger a company is, the less likely it is to fail. Sure, there have been some high-profile big company collapses in the past few decades but they've been few and far between. If you're a money nerd like me, you can probably count them on your fingers, and maybe your toes if you want to go beyond the year 2000.

I don't want to misrepresent the risk. If you invest in big companies your returns will still go up and down, but not as much as those for smaller companies.

Most investors who are new to the game think all shares have the same risk attached—that it's either a win-big or a lose-big bet. This may be the case if you speculate by investing in smaller companies, but when you choose to invest in the biggest and best companies, speculating becomes investing.

The next obvious question is how do you find and invest in the biggest and most stable companies in the world? The good news is that's exactly what you get when you invest in index funds.

What is an index fund?

An index fund tracks the overall share market. The ASX200 is the index of the 200 largest companies listed on the Australian Stock Exchange, and its combined value at 31 January 2024 was $2.62 trillion.

Figure 4.1 breaks down the biggest companies. BHP, the largest company in Australia, was valued at $222.8 billion at 31 January 2024, which meant it accounted for 8.50 per cent of the total value of the ASX200.

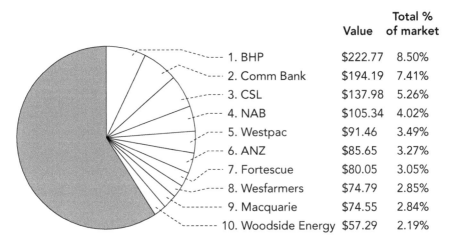

	Value	Total % of market
1. BHP	$222.77	8.50%
2. Comm Bank	$194.19	7.41%
3. CSL	$137.98	5.26%
4. NAB	$105.34	4.02%
5. Westpac	$91.46	3.49%
6. ANZ	$85.65	3.27%
7. Fortescue	$80.05	3.05%
8. Wesfarmers	$74.79	2.85%
9. Macquarie	$74.55	2.84%
10. Woodside Energy	$57.29	2.19%

Total value: AUD$2.62 trillion

Figure 4.1 ASX200 company values

An ASX200 index fund invests money in the same percentages and proportions as apply to the share market itself, so the return on an ASX200 index fund is almost identical to the return on the share market.

When you invest in an index fund, most of your investing will go into the biggest companies listed on exchanges around the world. On the flip side, while you do still have some exposure to smaller companies, this exposure is limited.

Because index funds use technology to make sure their investments remain aligned with the market, these funds are also low cost. This means more of the fund investment returns are added to your bottom line rather than evaporating as fees and charges.

Active vs passive investing

There are really only two ways to invest: active or passive. With active investing, either you or a professional fund manager picks investments that will perform better than the share market as a whole. Passive investing simply tracks the overall market and targets its average return.

There are a lot of different ways to be right when it comes to investing. Every approach to investing has an upside, and if you look at enough examples you'll find someone who has made money investing in weird and wonderful ways, but some ways are 'more right' than others.

According to research from S&P Indices Versus Active (SPIVA), passive index funds perform better than active investments more than 80 per cent of the time. This means if you choose active over passive, the odds will be stacked against you eight times out of ten.

Particularly for Virgin Millionaires, a crucial element to success at each of the Smart Money Stages is consistent progress.

You don't need to do anything crazy to get some pretty insane results; you just need to take action and get started investing and consistently add to your investments over time. This is a good time to review table 1.3 from chapter 1 (on page xx), which shows how much you need to save and invest to reach your wealth goal. Note that the table assumes you receive only the average share market return of 9.8 per cent, which just happens to be the return on an index fund investment.

The upside of active investing is the potential to achieve returns in excess of the market. You could in theory get a return of 15 per cent compared to the market return of 9.8 per cent.

If such a return were possible, table 4.1 shows how much you'd need to save and invest to hit the same targets.

Table 4.1 how investments grow assuming 15 per cent annual return

		Age							
		20	25	30	35	40	45	50	55
Daily saving to build wealth by age 65	$1m investments ($50k income)	$0.50	$1.06	$2.24	$4.75	$10.14	$21.96	$49.18	$119.46
	$1.5m investments ($75k income)	$0.75	$1.59	$3.36	$7.12	$15.20	$32.94	$73.77	$179.19
	$2m investments ($100k income)	$1.00	$2.12	$4.48	$9.50	$20.27	$43.92	$98.36	$238.91
	$2.5m investments ($125k income)	$1.26	$2.65	$5.60	$11.87	$25.34	$54.89	$122.95	$298.64
	$3m investments ($150k income)	$1.51	$3.18	$6.72	$14.25	$30.41	$65.87	$147.54	$358.37
	$4m investments ($200k income)	$2.01	$4.24	$8.96	$18.99	$40.54	$87.83	$196.72	$477.83
	$5m investments ($250k income)	$2.51	$5.30	$11.20	$23.74	$50.68	$109.79	$245.89	$597.28

That you'll need to invest a lot less to reach the same investment level makes this option attractive. But many new investors don't think about or don't fully understand the risks when they start down the active investing path.

On the pathway to becoming a Virgin Millionaire, momentum is crucial. You need to get started with saving and investing and get your momentum building. Then you simply need to keep it going, and let time and compounding do their thing.

It's important that bad or underperforming investments don't kill that momentum. An investment failure costs money, but much worse, it costs time as you make up lost ground just to be where you were before.

One of my favourite things about index fund investing is that an index fund can go to zero only if every single company goes bust at the same time. In the Australian context, our biggest companies are the banks, supermarkets, utilities and mining companies. Imagine every bank, supermarket, telco provider and mining company going bankrupt at the same time.

It's a scary thought, because life as we know it would change. If it were to happen, we would face much bigger problems than the balance of your investment portfolio.

When should you move beyond index funds?

If index funds are such a great way to invest, why would you move beyond them? The short answer is you don't need to.

In the next chapter I cover sexy investments like crypto or gold and discuss how there is a place for them in a smart investing strategy. But they're not necessary. If you were to live your whole life investing only in index funds you'd get epic results, maybe even better than any other approach, as Warren Buffett has demonstrated.

Confidence is key to action

When you follow an index fund investing strategy, you can sleep like a baby knowing the money you have invested is as safe as it can be. The risks are low because the share market will do what the share market has always done: it will have ups and downs, but it will trend upward over the medium to long term.

The confidence that comes from choosing index funds reduces your fear and puts you in a position to take action and invest more money sooner and to do it more consistently over a longer period.

If you're investing actively, you have to spend a heap more time doing your due diligence, choosing your investments or investment managers, looking at track records and performance. But still the odds will be stacked against you.

If you invest in non-index funds, you are more likely to react when the share market goes through a period of turbulence or when it's on a downward trend. When the market starts wobbling, it's not unusual for an active investor to suffer a mild panic attack.

Many sell to slow or stop losses, but a downturn is the worst time to attempt this because you're effectively locking in a loss. It's also common to then sit on the sidelines until things go back to normal, which means missing out on the strongest part of the market recovery.

To put some numbers around this, I've drawn on some market analysis from Australian investment powerhouse Pearler. They found that if you'd invested $10k in the 500 largest US companies (S&P500) 30 years ago, your investment would today be worth around $208k, reflecting a total return of 1980 per cent.

But if you weren't in the market on its 30 best days over that same 30-year period, your $10k would be worth $36k today, $172k *less*.

The surprising thing is that more than 83 per cent of the best days happened either during or immediately following bear market periods when the share market had declined by 20 per cent or more.

The lesson is that if you're not investing consistently, and particularly during market downturns, your investments won't grow as much or as quickly as you want them to. If you take an active investment approach, you're much more likely to either fully sit out or invest less during downturns, and that will cost you a lot of money.

Always be investing

This may be controversial, but in my opinion every single person (and most definitely every Virgin Millionaire) should always be investing. And this is regardless of what's going on in the markets, with your money or in the world.

Investing is a muscle you build and a skill you get better at with every investment you make. Whether you're right at the start of your Virgin Millionaire journey, or whether you're in a tight spot from a savings capacity perspective, or a heap of other things are holding you back, you should still be investing regularly. And I say this with the current cost-of-living crisis very much front of mind.

Today some investing accounts allow you to invest with as little as a single cent, and almost all of them allow you to invest $5 at a time. No matter how tight your budget, investing $5 regularly will make you feel so much better than you would if you invested nothing. And you'll continue to build the investing knowledge and skills that will benefit you in the years ahead when you'll be able to invest more.

My challenge is that you commit to investing regularly. Your fallback position is $5 a week, which will help you build your investing knowledge, skills and confidence. You can afford $5 a week regardless of what else is going on with your money. This baseline will help you to focus on investing forever, on learning and on building your investor muscle.

According to the Australian Stock Exchange 2023 investor survey, 49 per cent of Australians have never invested outside their super fund or their own home if they're home owners. So by investing even $5 a day, you'll be doing better than almost half of all Australians. That's something to feel good about as you frame your mindset to nail your Virgin Millionaire journey.

There will be periods when you'll be investing more, but this small, regular investment amount is your new baseline.

Types of investments

Ultimately there are a few different types of share-based investments to be across, and choosing the right option at the right time is an important part of making good progress on your Virgin Millionaire journey.

Shares

The oldest and simplest form of investing is referred to as investing into direct shares. When you buy a share, you're buying up a small slice of a specific company. Your investment return will come from two areas. First, as the company grows over time its value will increase, as will the value of your share in the company. The second return comes when the company distributes profits or dividends to its shareholders.

One of the main advantages of investing in direct shares is that you can choose one or a few specific companies. This way, if the company you choose performs well, you'll benefit directly.

The main downside is your investments aren't diversified. This means your investment value can be subject to some big ups and downs and should your chosen company fail, the value of your investment will drop to zero.

Investing in direct shares is an active investment approach because you are actively choosing the shares you believe will perform best for you as opposed to tracking the market overall.

The investments I'll now cover are all pooled investments based on shares. Your money is pooled with that of other investors following a predetermined investment approach.

Diversification

Diversification is one of the most effective ways to reduce investment risk. It sounds jargony and complicated but it simply means spreading your risk. Consider this example:

If you invest in only one company, your returns will be reliant on that company. If it performs well your investment value will increase but if it performs poorly your investment value will decline.

As soon as you invest in a second company, your total return becomes the *average* of their return. You'll have diversified your investments.

(*continued*)

Figure 4.2 shows that as soon as you have two investments in your portfolio, the lows of one are balanced by the highs of the other. You'll experience fewer ups and downs.

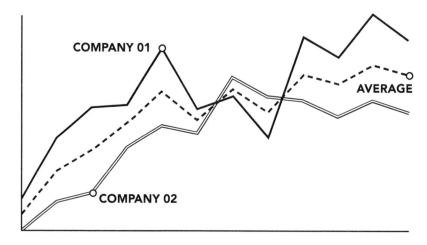

Figure 4.2 the effect of diversification

The more investments you have in your portfolio, the more diversified it will be and the less impact any one company's results will have on your overall return. As I've discussed, there are a lot of different ways to be right when you invest, but in my opinion you should aim for a highly diversified investment portfolio. This will let you 'diversify away' any company-specific risk and you'll be left with the overall share market risk, which is exactly the risk you want. This market risk is the risk that will make you money as an investor.

When you're investing in shares directly, you diversify by buying individual shares in different companies. When you invest through any of the pooled investment options I'll discuss now, you can diversify by holding a single investment.

Managed funds

A managed fund is a pool of money contributed by a group of investors and managed by a professional fund manager. This person or company invests the money in line with a specific mandate or strategy.

There are thousands of managed funds out there, ranging from index funds that simply track the market, to funds that invest only in specific sectors like mining, technology, agriculture, and almost anything else you can think of.

The big advantage of managed funds is that you have only to choose one managed fund, which in turn invests into a range of shares. You get the benefits of diversification without having to do the work.

Investing in a pool also spreads the ongoing administration and investing costs so they will generally be lower than running a large direct share portfolio yourself.

There are two main downsides to managed funds. First, they can only be accessed on an investment platform or directly from a managed fund provider, so the admin to set up and actually invest money can be a bit of a pain. That said, technology is making this easier and better, and managed fund investing is likely to get easier and cheaper with time.

The second downside is more complicated and revolves around the tax on managed fund investing. The technical side is fairly complex, but the short version is that investing taxes like capital gains and losses are spread across all investors within each managed fund.

This means that even if you have only ever bought and never sold investments in a managed fund, because other investors are buying and selling all the time, you will pay capital gains tax on the gains made by others in your fund. But until you have several hundred thousand dollars in a managed fund the tax impact is unlikely to make a material difference to the bottom line of your investment account balance.

Once you progress through your Smart Money Stages there will be a tax impact, and when you get up to seven figures in wealth the tax consequences of this sort of structure can be prohibitive.

In short, managed funds can be good if you find a good provider, but in my opinion there are better options out there for most investors.

Exchange-traded funds (ETFs)

ETFs have become hugely popular since their launch in 2001, and for good reason. ETFs are bought and sold like shares on the stock exchange through a broker, online trading platform or investment app but are a pooled investment similar to managed funds. You purchase one ETF, which in turn invests into a number of underlying shares, giving you instant diversification.

The big advantage of ETFs over managed funds and other pooled investments is that you have more control over tax outcomes. This gets a little complicated, but the short version is that when you buy an ETF, such as an ASX200 ETF, you are effectively buying a small slice of the 200 largest companies in Australia.

There are no tax implications until you sell, no matter how long you hold your ETF and no matter what other investors in the same ETF are doing. This is because in an ETF you own your small slice of these 200 shares individually.

Because of this control of tax outcomes, along with the ease of access, ETFs are one of my favourite investments.

The main downside is that because ETFs need to be purchased as a trade on the stock exchange, there are transaction costs. These brokerage costs can eat into your investment funds and thus into your returns, particularly if you're only investing small amounts of money.

Micro-investing

Micro-investing is a recent innovation in the investment landscape, and entered the scene only around a decade ago. It has become one of the most popular ways to invest and there are millions of micro-investors across the country.

What has driven its rise is you can start small. Some micro-investing platforms (such as Sharesies) allow you to get started with as little as a single cent and almost all the others allow you to kick off with as little as $5. This is a game changer for investors who previously needed to meet a minimum investment requirement in the hundreds of dollars to access an investment fund or index fund–type investment.

The other big benefit of micro-investing is that the technology makes getting started easy. Financial institutions and investing companies have been notorious for their clunky user experience and complicated and annoying paperwork. But because they were the only ones in the market, investors had no other options. Micro-investing has changed the game.

Because micro-investing wasn't built on historical bank systems, companies have been able to focus on a streamlined user experience more in line with that of a tech company. You can typically set up an account for free with a few swipes and clicks on your phone and be investing in under 15 minutes.

At first micro-investing was the place for new investors to get started and wasn't sufficiently competitive for more established investors. But as the costs of micro-investing platforms have come down and the range of options has increased, these platforms have gained a broader appeal.

Choosing between the options

I've explained each of the key investing options, but don't worry if your head is spinning. Your choice will be fairly simple.

First, keep in mind that investing in direct shares is quite different from the other investment options, because when you invest in direct shares you're choosing to put all your investing money into one or a small number of companies. This means you're choosing to be an active investor.

The other options are pooled investments in which you purchase one investment option that holds a number of different shares. Given the power of diversification, it's worth noting you can only follow an index fund or passive investing strategy by choosing a pooled investment option like an ETF, managed fund or micro-investing platform.

Because of the lack of diversification that comes with investing in direct shares, and the fact that statistically an active investment approach is less effective, I typically suggest avoiding investing in direct shares. If you're interested in direct shares, I suggest this as an advanced strategy to consider once you've made some progress into the later Smart Money Stages. I discuss this further in chapter 5.

If you're aligned with diversified investing, the question becomes which option, ETF, micro-investing or managed funds, will be best for you? The answer is simple.

It doesn't (really) matter.

This may be contentious and lose me a few brownie points with my buddies in personal finance, but it's true, particularly if you want to invest in index funds and you're early in your Virgin Millionaire journey. This is because the actual dollar difference will be almost zero.

Table 4.2 compares a managed fund and an ETF. For this example I've used the Vanguard Australian Share Index investment, which offers both an ETF and managed-fund option.

Table 4.2 return on managed funds vs ETFs

	1 year	3 years (p.a.)	5 years (p.a.)	10 years (p.a.)
Fund return (%)	10.40	9.03	8.56	7.82
ETF return (%)	10.50	9.10	8.62	7.88
Difference (%)	0.10	0.07	0.06	0.06
Annual difference on $100k invested	$100	$70	$60	$60

You can see from these figures that the return on ETF is slightly higher across all time periods. That said, when you look at the actual dollar impact in the final line of the table, you can see that for every $100000 you have invested, the difference in returns is less than $100 p.a.

It's only really when your investment exceeds $500000 that you'll even notice the difference.

In terms of your long-term investment strategy, when it comes to pooled investments you would be wise to choose ETFs because when you have millions of dollars invested, the extra control you will have over tax outcomes will make a difference to your returns.

But ETFs aren't the best place to get started, mainly because it's difficult and expensive to automate ETF investing if you're not investing several hundreds or thousands of dollars at a time.

Micro-investing or managed funds are generally a better place to start not only because they allow for smaller minimum investments and have low investment 'buy' costs, but because investing through these accounts is easy to automate. Most managed-fund providers use clunky technology and require higher minimum regular investment amounts than micro-investment platforms do. Most new investors will find micro-investing an easy place to build your early investing momentum.

If you're on board with this approach, your question becomes when is micro-investing best and when do you make the shift to investing with ETFs?

When you're investing, any investment account you choose needs to meet certain criteria. Some of these are obvious, but it pays to follow a checklist when choosing an investment provider:

1. The account should be free to open.
2. The account should provide you with access to the investments you want today.
3. The fees should compare favourably with those of other similar accounts.
4. It should be easy to automate your investing.
5. Any minimum investment amount should be consistent with how much you plan to invest.

Because there isn't a huge difference between the financial outcomes across different types of investing accounts, the most important thing is ease of access and ease of automation. When investing is easy you will invest more and this will add more money to your bottom-line profit.

If you find an account that meets the criteria outlined above, know that this is a solid option that will boost your investing, regardless of whether you choose ETFs, micro-investing, managed funds or some combination of these options.

I've spoken to so many people who get caught up trying to choose the perfect investment account. Because they want to make the best decision, they waste a heap of time delaying their actual investing while they compare ETFs with managed funds with micro-investing.

The costs of delay can be high, so please don't let this happen to you.

Smart Money Stages and investing

Table 4.3 summarises investing success outcomes at each Smart Money Stage.

Table 4.3 Smart Money Stages and investing

Success outcomes	Foundations	Focus	Optimise	Accelerate	Impact
Investing	Have a regular investment plan for shares with automated weekly/ monthly contributions.	Invest a minimum 5 per cent of gross household income in shares.	Invest a minimum 10 per cent of gross household income in shares.	Achieve a net investment income equal to the Australian average income.	Achieve a net investment income equal to double the Australian average income, with income plan if employment ceased today.

Investing: Foundations

When you're at the Foundations stage, you're just getting started with your money. You should be aiming to set up a regular weekly investment plan as soon as possible.

The first step is to be crystal clear about the investment strategy you intend to adopt. Will you follow a passive index fund strategy or an active investment approach. As discussed, there are many ways to make the 'right' choice, but keep in mind that the statistics tell us index investing wins well over 80 per cent of the time. It's my own personal approach, and I believe it's the best strategy for most people.

When choosing your investment strategy, you need to focus on building enough confidence to follow through on this approach regardless of share market conditions or what's going on in the economy. This way, you'll be all set to sustain your regular investing week in and week out, all the way on your journey through the Smart Money Stages.

At the Foundations stage your regular investment plan will help you gain traction and start building momentum. But much more important than the actual money this investing will return is the habit you're building of investing regularly and consistently for the long term. Further, when you start investing at this stage you'll start building your knowledge, skills and confidence, all of which will pay dividends in the years to come.

Because you're likely starting investing with a small amount—potentially as little as a $5 regular investment—you'll want to use a suitable account. In my opinion, for most people micro-investing is a sensible starting point. Accounts are free to set up, most have low fees and all allow you to automate your investing easily so it happens magically on autopilot.

At this stage, the cost of financial advice will probably be too high relative to its value for you. However, educating yourself will be highly valuable so deserving of your time and attention.

You've made a great start (in my biased opinion) by picking up this book. If you need more of a push, you can download further free training at bit.ly/virginmillionaire, or if you need more of a push consider a short money education course. Your investment of time, and perhaps a small amount of money, will pay dividends.

Investing: Focus

At the Focus stage, you're building up your regular investing to at least 5 per cent of your household income. This is substantial and will start delivering some real financial traction and results.

Depending on your income and how interested you are in the investing space you may want to consider transitioning to ETF investing but this will only make sense if you're investing $500 or more a week or you have $100k or more in investments already. Even then, it's probably a line-ball call. Micro-investing is still likely to be a solid option that will help you keep building your investing momentum.

As your investments increase, it may be time to consider a financial adviser to support your progress.

Investing: Optimise

At the Optimise stage, your aim is to build your regular investments to 10 per cent of your household income. You're getting into the territory of fairly substantial investing.

You should be starting to consider the transition to ETF investing, particularly if you're investing $1000 or more weekly, or have more than $200k in investments, or both. At this level, ETFs will give you an extra level of control over tax outcomes. While this wouldn't have made much of a difference before now, as your investments build, tax starts to have a greater impact, so controlling this is key.

Before changing investments, take the time to read chapter 8 on tax planning to make sure you get the best after-tax return on the money you have invested.

If you're interested, this is the time you could consider more sexy investments like startups or crypto (see following chapter). I will add the caveat that you don't need these sorts of investments in the mix, but you can do this now, carefully, without seriously jeopardising your results.

At this stage your money momentum should be building nicely. If you're concerned you may be missing something, consider bringing in an adviser. They will likely identify opportunities for you to make more money from the money you have, but even if they don't they'll give you confidence to crack on.

Investing: Accelerate

At the Accelerate stage you'll be building real momentum around your investments. You will have tens of thousands of dollars in investment income each year, and your target will be an investment income equal to the average Australian income.

Tax planning and tax optimisation should be rock solid at the Accelerate stage. If you haven't already done so, seek out professional advice to help you with investment strategies and tax planning and optimisation. The cost of advice will pay for itself several times over.

Most likely current and future investment contributions will be directed towards ETFs to deliver more control over your tax outcomes and planning.

Investing: Impact

By now your money dream team will be providing high-calibre support to your investing strategy, tax planning and optimisation, as well as to your intergenerational legacy and giving strategies.

Because everyone's version of true financial independence and money success is different, there's no one right approach to investing at the Impact stage. But there are principles worth following:

- Your investments should be delivering, at a minimum, enough income to fund your ideal lifestyle.
- Your investment income should be tax effective, leveraging strategies like franking credits.
- You should have an investment by entity strategy, owning the right investments in the right tax structures.

At this Smart Money Stage, you will have a large amount of money behind you, allowing you to choose among a heap of good options. The greatest impact comes when you choose the path that delivers the right investment outcomes in line with your ideal lifestyle plan.

THE WRAP

Investing is the key to not having to work forever. The sooner you start investing, the less work you'll need to put in over time. You now know that one of the most important drivers of investing success is to avoid missteps and investment failures. And you have a solid understanding of how to avoid costly investing mistakes.

Investing can seem complicated, and this is magnified by all the noise out there around the smartest investing moves. But in reality, the principles of successful investing are simple: choose good investments, invest as much as you can as quickly as you can, and don't risk being forced to sell at a bad time.

Keep in mind that the right move becomes the wrong one if the timing's wrong. Your next move needs to be right for the stage you're at. This way you'll find the fastest path through the five stages to reach true money success and smart money freedom.

Take action

- [ ] Get clear on big vs small company risk and how this can drive more confidence in your investing.

- [ ] Re-read the section on index funds and do further research to see where these fit for you.

- [ ] Choose your investment strategy: active or passive.

- [ ] Understand the power of compounding over the long term and why it's so important to get started now.

- [ ] Do enough research to take your first (or next) step to invest more money today.

- [ ] Leverage the learnings from this chapter on the power of diversification and the importance of including this at the centre of your investing strategy.

- [ ] Understand the difference between ETFs, micro-investing and index funds, but know that it only really matters when you've got $500k+ so don't get stalled choosing.

- [ ] Choose the investment account you're going to use in the short term and set it up. Bonus points for setting up an automatic investment right from the start.

CHAPTER 5

Sexy investing

When you've got big goals for your money, or when you're on a strong path with your savings and investments, it's natural to start thinking about less traditional areas for investment.

You'll have come across stories about people who have made big money investing in, for example, startup companies, cryptocurrency, buying gold and precious metals, and trading currencies.

In this chapter I refer to investments outside the spheres of established share investments (including ETFs and funds), residential property or cash and term deposits as sexy. Clearly this isn't a technical label, but you get the point.

These investments sound exciting, so you look further. You find quite a few people are talking about them as *the* way to make serious money in a relatively short time. Because your inner investor craves big returns as quickly as possible, these stories have an inbuilt psychological appeal.

And this is where it can all go wrong.

The first million dollars you make is the hardest million you'll ever make. Consider this example.

Starting with $0 in investments and saving then investing $25 a day, and assuming a long-term share market return of 9.8 per cent, it would take just over 25 years to build your first million. While this is a great outcome, it has taken a long time as well as serious focus and work.

From there, things get easier.

Once you've built your first million, if you save and invest at exactly the same rate of $25 a day, you'll build your second million dollars in just six years. If you keep going with the same rate of savings and investing, your third million will be yours in only four years.

This happens because in building your first million, you've created the momentum that will do a lot of the heavy lifting to achieve your next million. And it gets better...

If you continue to save and invest at exactly the same rate, you will build your fourth million in only three years and your fifth million in two and if you keep saving at exactly the same rate of $25 a day, your investments will grow by $1 million every single year.

Your momentum is seriously cranking up.

This shows how powerful investing momentum is and how important it is to keep this progress going. The biggest risk to this progress is choosing bad investments that fail.

Not only will your momentum be stalled but you'll lose money and be forced to put in more work and time to rebuild.

Sexy investments can have a place on your Virgin Millionaire journey, but making the wrong choice is a big risk to your progress.

I'll now unpack the most common types of sexy investment and how they work so you can make an informed decision about their place in your investment strategy.

Cryptocurrency

In the past 10 years the total value of all cryptocurrency (crypto) has increased over 28 900 per cent from less than US$8 billion to US$2.48 trillion today. Crypto like Bitcoin is tipped to continue to rise strongly in the years ahead.

What's driving the popularity of cryptocurrency?

The basis of most crypto such as Bitcoin and other digital assets is blockchain, which is essentially a decentralised digital ledger that has been around since 1991. Bitcoin was launched in 2009 and since then its popularity has grown exponentially.

The ups and downs of crypto have been marked since its inception but its long-term upward trajectory is clear. In recent years in particular we've seen its adoption by a number of high-profile companies, including Tesla and PayPal, as a form of payment. This validation is shifting public opinion, and people of all ages are investing in increasing numbers.

Another factor driving the growth of crypto is ups and downs of share markets in Australia and around the world over the past few years, coupled with low then high interest rates and the global inflation crisis. Investors are looking for alternative places to invest their savings, and the rise in the value of cryptocurrency has put it in the spotlight.

What are the risks with buying cryptocurrency?

All investments come with risk; after all, risk is what makes you money. Investing in crypto is risky, but so is buying shares and property; even doing nothing comes with its own risks.

But given the unregulated nature and complexity of cryptocurrency markets, there are particular risks to be across if you're thinking about jumping on the digital crypto bandwagon.

Volatility, or ups and downs in the value of crypto, is significantly higher than for traditional investments. This volatility is driven by a number of factors including positive and negative news about market prices, as well as the fact that a large crypto investor's need to sell their position (or buy more) can move the market and change prices significantly. Security breaches and crypto seizures are other significant price drivers.

Another key risk is the fact that crypto doesn't pay an income and your first big goal as an investor is to grow an investment income that can replace your salary. You will benefit from investing in cryptocurrency only when you sell.

The next risk is that crypto like Bitcoin is held in a digital wallet, which means it is being minded by someone else. An Australian share portfolio, on the other hand, is held by a company regulated under the Australian financial market regulator APRA, so there is next to no risk your investments will go missing. A number of crypto exchanges are based overseas, which can mean that if something goes wrong it can be harder for you to chase down your cash.

Finally, because cryptocurrency is digital, it's vulnerable to hackers. This risk is amplified by the fact that data (from trend watchers like Cardify) show over a third of crypto investors don't fully understand the technology. This means this particular risk is very real, and one you will need to manage if you're thinking about joining the crypto-buyer's club.

Gold and precious metals

Gold is an investment that people have been drawn to throughout human history and remains the most valuable investment (by total value) in the world today. It's no surprise that this asset attracts the attention of investors, but there is a lot of noise that surrounds gold. Here I'll cover the key things you really need to know.

Benefits of investing in gold

The huge increase in the price of gold in recent years has captured the attention of investors. From 2000 to 2024 its value has increased by over 649 per cent, but it's important to keep in mind how this compares with other investments.

The most relevant comparison is the value of shares. Over the same period the S&P500 (the 500 largest stocks on the US stock market) increased in value by 185 per cent but there have been periods in which shares have performed much more strongly than gold. For example, since 2010 the price of gold has increased by 42 per cent while shares have increased by over 262 per cent. This makes it clear that while gold has performed well over the long term, so have other investments — and that when you 'cherry pick' periods in time for comparing investments, it's easy to make something appear better than it is.

Another big advantage of investing in gold is that it tends to move differently from the share market. When shares go down through a large market correction or a crash, gold tends to increase in value. This means the overall investment return is less volatile for an investor who holds both shares and gold.

What are the risks?

Like crypto, a downside of gold is that it doesn't generate income. You don't receive any financial return until you sell. This means gold is *not* a good investment for someone looking to build a second passive income from investments.

Another risk is volatility. Gold can experience much bigger, and more stressful, price swings than more traditional investments like shares or property.

This might work in your favour when gold prices are going up, but it can work against you when prices are going down.

If you're looking to buy gold, you want to own a gold bar, or at least a small slice of one, so you need to think about how you will actually buy your gold and how you will manage it. There are two main options.

First, you can buy physical gold. This means you'll either store it yourself or pay someone to store it for you. Clearly there are associated risks. You don't want to lose your gold bar or have someone steal it. And there are challenges when you come to realise your investment. You will need to physically exchange the gold for money.

Second, you can buy gold through an ETF (exchange-traded fund) or managed investment fund. A professional fund manager and gold buyer will source your gold, store it and manage the administration, investment and tax reporting on your behalf.

A big advantage of the second option is that there is an active public market for your investment so it's easy to buy and sell your gold investment, which can be done in smaller parcels.

Bonds

The tightening in interest rates has come with no small amount of pain and discomfort for many Australians.

This has been good for investors in that interest rates on cash and cash-based savings accounts have gone through the roof. In early 2024 you could buy bonds backed by the US Government that paid an annual return of 10 per cent. This has led many investors to consider whether bonds have a role to play in their investing strategy.

But for the previous decade or so the return on bonds has been close to 0 per cent, so for good reason they've not been popular. If you're new to the investing game, or even if you've been at it for a while, you're probably wondering what these investments are all about and how to figure out if they're a smart move for you.

What are bonds?

Bonds are like a term deposit on steroids; you agree to park your savings for an agreed period and in exchange you are promised a set interest rate. The interest rate can be fixed or variable, and some pay a return based on the rate of inflation.

Why would you want to invest in bonds?

Inflation-linked bonds are delivering high returns now, with sky-high inflation internationally. A bond that's paying a 4 to 5 per cent return might sound okay, but if it's paying this same rate on top of the inflation rate it's a game changer.

The big benefit of bonds is that they pay a consistent return and aren't subject to the ups and downs of the share market. Bonds are typically secured by the bond issuer, which is to say that whoever issues the bond guarantees to repay the money plus the promised interest rate.

Further, whoever issues the bond puts up assets as collateral to back it. This means bonds are typically more stable than shares or property.

When you get to the point where you've built your wealth and investments, bonds can be a secure way to achieve a solid income.

What are the risks?

The first is that the company or institution that issues the bond will default. If the issuer is someone like the US Government, this risk is fairly low, but bonds are issued by companies of all shapes and sizes. If you buy bonds in, say, a small startup, the risk can be significant.

When you invest in bonds, you need to be confident the issuer is going to be around to make the interest payments and return your money when the bond comes due.

Another risk is fluctuations in the price and value of bonds over time. While bonds are typically more stable than other investments, their value can fluctuate. If you have a bond that's paying a set rate, when interest rates go up or down new bonds created may pay a higher or lower rate than the one you hold. This will reduce, or increase, the price someone would pay for yours.

A lot of investors were caught out by these price fluctuations through 2023 as interest rates increased globally. They thought they were buying a stable investment, but as interest rates increased, the value of older bonds was pummelled because no investors wanted to buy existing bonds as they were paying a lower return. So bond investing does not guarantee security of the value of your money.

The biggest risk with investing in bonds is that they are income as opposed to growth investments. They pay a set income return until your capital is returned at the end of the term. Because your money doesn't grow while it's sitting in the bond, inflation can take a large chunk out of your real return.

For example, if you'd bought a bond in 2022 that was being paid back in 2024, high inflation over those 24 months would mean its buying power would be much lower than it was when you kicked off your investment.

Further, in Australia the income paid on bond investments is taxable, so your after-tax return is much lower than the headline interest rate. This means that over the long term the after-tax and after-inflation return on bonds is typically very low (less than 2 per cent), and much lower than the after-tax and -inflation return on investments like shares.

Startup investing

The strong allure of startups is driven largely by stories of those who have made large piles of money by investing in early-stage companies, along with the fact that some of the world's richest people made their money from new businesses that took off.

What is startup investing?

The most common way to invest in startups is through buying shares in the company itself. Because such companies won't yet be listed on the stock exchange, the way you buy these shares will be a little different.

Startups usually sell shares directly to investors when they're raising capital to help fund operations and growth.

If a new company wants to launch to market, or if a young company wants to add a new product or service or to grow its existing operations, they will likely need cash. If they cannot fund these activities themselves, they will look to outside investors to exchange cash for shares in the company.

How to invest in startups

Unlike buying a share on the publicly accessible and publicly traded share market, buying a share in a startup is typically a private transaction. However, increasing numbers of platforms are connecting startups looking to raise capital with investors who want to try their hand at startup investing.

The most common platforms for startup investing are Equitise, Birchal and VentureCrowd, and in the US the biggest players are StartEngine and OurCrowd. They make startup investing more accessible by running the admin and finance side of the investment, and some of them even perform a vetting process for the companies looking to list on their platform.

What are the risks?

Investing in small companies is riskier than investing in bigger companies. Small companies are typically new and therefore have no track record. They have less diversified operations and fewer income streams, so internal or external risks can challenge future growth.

Many startup companies have solid internal controls and processes but because, they are not subject to the strict standards of governance and regulation that apply to public companies, they may be more vulnerable to risk. When a company is publicly listed, it's required to appoint a formal board, to report regularly on all areas of its finances and to bring in external auditors to review operations and ensure everything is as it should be.

When a company looks to raise capital by selling shares, they effectively set the price at what they think the company is worth or what they think an investor might pay. This means that if they set the price at an overly optimistic level, even if the company does continue to grow it could take a long time for the true value of the company to catch up with the share price.

Like other investments discussed in this chapter, startup companies typically don't pay dividends either because they aren't yet profitable or because they want to reinvest profits in the company.

When you invest in a startup, you hope the company will ultimately list on the stock exchange as a publicly traded company. Until this happens, you can't actually sell your shares. You're playing a waiting game until the company makes it big.

Based on research conducted by the world's largest technology share market, Nasdaq, the average age of a company when it lists on the stock exchange is 11 years. As an investor in a startup, you're likely to have to wait a long time to get a return on your investment.

Where startup investing can go wrong

Dave was earning a good income and managing to save a solid amount with each pay cheque. He knew he should have been doing something smarter with his savings and he knew he was paying too much tax, but he didn't know what to do and didn't want to make a costly mistake.

After talking with his mates, who were serious investors in the startup investing space, he put most of his savings into an up-and-coming startup that had huge potential. The investment was growing as expected and Dave and his mates were very happy.

This all sounds great, right? Well, sort of.

The long and short of it is that Dave ended up smashing it at his job and getting a good pay bump (he knew this was on the cards and had been working towards it for a while). His increased income, together with a couple of other strategies we had set up, meant he ended up in a position to buy his first property much sooner than he had thought possible.

But this is where the challenge came in.

All these things on their own are great. Investments doing well. More savings. Less tax. More income. Able to buy property. But Dave was effectively locked into the startup investment until it listed on the stock exchange in a few years. He was unable to get his money out or take the profits he needed to use as the deposit on the property he wanted to buy.

His only option was to hold off until he'd saved up the deposit.

Increases in Sydney property values meant that by the time Dave had enough cash to buy, he could afford a lot less for the same money. His startup investment had made money on paper but because he couldn't cash out and buy property sooner, the cost of waiting to buy property was higher than the money he made on his startup investment.

Commercial property

Commercial property is all property that's not residential. It includes retail premises, office buildings, factories, warehouses and everything in between. The benefit of investing in commercial property is that rents are generally higher than they are for regular residential investment properties.

Another reason commercial property is popular with investors who have a lot of money is that the value of commercial properties can be a lot higher than that of standard residential properties. This means that if you have a lot of money, you can save work and administration by taking on a single investment worth several million dollars as opposed to managing several residential properties.

How to invest in commercial property

Commercial property is bought and sold in the same way as residential property. It's listed for sale on the market, usually through a specialist commercial real-estate agent.

The risks

The first risk of investing with commercial property is that your tenant will generally be a business, and if the business doesn't do well your rental income can be at risk. Changing tenants typically takes longer because the property needs to be set up specifically for the occupier.

Because the value of a commercial property is linked closely to the economic cycle, values can be volatile. When the economy is going well and businesses are growing, commercial property values go up, but when the economy struggles values generally come down. With residential property, values tend to be driven purely by supply and demand.

Where sexy investments fit for smart investors

By now you know enough to understand what you should look out for if you're considering sexy investing. But, as always, the million-dollar question is are these investments right for you? And if so, which will work best?

In my opinion, no one needs to invest in these areas. Ever.

If you go through your whole life never investing a single dollar in the kinds of investments covered in this chapter, you can comfortably become a Virgin Millionaire. In fact, you will probably get there faster with less work and less stress.

But there is money to be made here if you make the right move at the right time. The right move for you depends on the stage you're currently at with your money, so I'll now unpack sexy investments and what makes a smart and not-so-smart move in relation to your Smart Money Stages.

First, there are a couple of things to watch regardless of the stage you're at.

No income is a serious challenge

One of the biggest investor protections when it comes to buying traditional shares and property investments is that when you choose quality investments you should consistently receive an income from them into the future.

You'll recall that, with the exception of bonds and commercial property, the investments discussed in this chapter don't provide an income. Given your aim is to reach smart money freedom, and by definition this means you have enough money in investments to fund your ideal lifestyle, if you have a heap of investments that *aren't* delivering any income they aren't helping you reach your goal.

Given that until you get to the final Smart Money Stage, when you'll have enough investment income to fund your ideal lifestyle, you will rely on investment income to either cover your living expenses, or reinvest to get ahead further, or some combination of both.

Even during a market downturn, most quality investments will continue to pay a return. For shares, this will take the form of dividends, which may be reduced but are unlikely to be cut altogether. With property investments, you'll receive your rent regardless of what's going on with the value of your property.

If investments are going through a period when they're down in value, the income you receive when investment markets and values are down can be used to invest more at lower prices to buffer the overall performance of your investments, ready for when markets and investment values recover.

Remember that without an income, you won't have extra money to invest. I see this as a serious problem and probably the biggest downside of sexy investments.

Investing doesn't need to be exciting

As you know from chapter 4, I'm a big advocate of investing both in index funds that track the share market and in quality residential properties in premium areas. These investments are rock solid and provide consistent growth and income returns.

I've advocated these investments with my clients for more than 15 years and in this time they've delivered life-changing results. But through this time I've had a number of pretty frank conversations with clients who start looking at investments outside of index funds and premium residential property because they want to spice up their investing and make it a bit more exciting.

And to be honest, on one level I agree with them. Index investing is a bit boring. So is buying up premium properties in blue-chip areas. But someone once shared a pearl of wisdom with me that's proved to be true time and time again.

Boring is profitable.

In my opinion, if you want excitement, play video games. If you want to make money, choose good investments.

Smart Money Stages and sexy investments

You now have a solid sense of the smart moves you need to make if you choose to make a sexy investment. As for all the other areas of your money we've talked about, your decision will depend on the Smart Money Stage you're at (table 5.1).

Table 5.1 Smart Money Stages and sexy investments

Success outcomes	Foundations	Focus	Optimise	Accelerate	Impact
Investing	Have a regular investment plan for shares with automated weekly/monthly contributions.	Invest minimum 5% gross household income in shares.	Invest minimum 10% gross household income in shares.	Net investment income equal to average Australian income.	Net investment income equal to double average Australian income, with income plan if employment ceased today.

Sexy investments: Foundations

At this stage, you're putting in place the Foundations of your long-term wealth. Just as you wouldn't build a house on top of a rollercoaster you won't build sexy investments into your financial foundations.

At the Foundations stage, you'll start getting serious about your money and recognise there is a long way to go. The temptation will be to look for shortcuts and speculative high-potential-return investments can seem appealing.

It's possible that if you were to include sexy investments in your strategy you will be one of the 0.000000001 per cent who hit a winner that accelerates their progress. But the much more likely outcome is that you blow the little cash you have to get started and block your momentum.

You'll have to play catch-up, sacrificing more and putting in more work just to get back to where you were. Because this risks your Virgin Millionaire progress, I suggest these investments should be avoided at all costs when you're at the Foundations stage.

Sexy investments: Focus

Your focus is to get into the property market. Once you buy your first solid investment property, you can use the power of leverage to accelerate your asset-building and wealth accumulation.

The financial upside benefits of this move are huge, and are the lead domino for a lot of the serious wealth-building options that will arise later. For this reason you should push to get there as quickly as you can, and avoid anything that might hold you back.

So in my opinion sexy investments should be avoided at the Focus stage.

Sexy investments: Optimise

At the Optimise stage you have a solid investment property behind you. By the end of this stage you should be investing 10 per cent of your income in share-type investments. If you're particularly keen to include sexy investments in your asset building as you move through this stage, you could consider including them in the mix without seriously compromising your progress.

However, should you make this choice you'll need to set clear controls and targets for a proportion of your money you can direct towards these more speculative investments.

As is the case so often with investment, there are a lot of ways to be right here but I would advise you to invest no more than 5 per cent of all new savings money, and you should preserve your existing investment mix. Don't sell down 5 per cent of your existing investments to make way for sexy investments. If you decide to include these investments in the mix, carve off 5 per cent of your new savings and use these instead.

You'll start introducing sexy investments in a controlled way without jeopardising your existing investing momentum.

Sexy investments: Accelerate

At this stage you're starting to build serious traction. You don't need sexy investments, but as you build out your rock-solid, boring-but-effective investment portfolio, these investments can be an interesting way to keep you learning and honing your skills.

There is a risk that if you start putting some of your money into sexy investments and you get lucky, you'll be tempted to push more of your investments into this area. Don't! Given how close you're getting to smart money freedom, your main job is to stay on track.

If you want to include these investments in the mix, keep your controls in place and ensure you never have more than 5 per cent of your total share investments in higher risk areas.

Sexy investments: Impact

At this point you can effectively do whatever you want—but this doesn't mean it's a smart idea.

You've arrived at true financial independence. Your investments allow you to live your ideal lifestyle today and every day into the future without having to work for a pay cheque.

It's important you maintain the solid and boring core investments that will continue to deliver your ideal lifestyle level of spending. Never shift any of the money in this bucket into sexy investments. But you will have a surplus money bucket, and you can invest that money where you choose.

If you choose sexy investments, know that any dollar you put into this bucket could go to zero and limit your exposure. But ultimately the point of true freedom is that you can do anything you really want to, so if you want to invest in crypto or precious metals, then go for gold.

THE WRAP

Sexy investments have a deep subconscious appeal to every investor, driven by the fact we love thinking about the potential to make a boatload of money fast. But the reality is that huge upside potential comes with massive downside risk.

With time on your side, you don't need to do a lot to become a Virgin Millionaire. It's all about building momentum and keeping it up. Your main job on this path is avoiding the missteps and mistakes that lead to momentum-killing setbacks. And sexy investments are one of the most common traps.

You don't need sexy investments, and they probably won't make you any more money than traditional property- and share-based investments. But if you are tempted, you can include them in your investment mix without excessive risk. The key is ensuring you're mindful of the Smart Money Stage you're at, and the right moves for that stage.

If you do this, the result will be steady progress, consistent results, and ultimately more peace of mind on your Virgin Millionaire journey.

Take action

- Know that you don't *need* any of the investments covered in this chapter.

- Understand the gravity of the 'no income' risk that comes with sexy investments and the impact this will have on your progress to future freedom.

- Think about whether sexy investing is something that's really important to you and, if it is, what's driving this so you can plan your future investing moves.

- If you really want to include sexy investments in your strategy, make a decision around which Smart Money Stage you feel this best fits and what percentage of your new investments you want to direct to these investments.

- Recognise that while some sexy investments have good short-term return figures that are spruiked by marketers, over the long term more traditional investments perform better.

CHAPTER 6

Why rich people need a budget (the most)

To make money when you invest, do two simple things. Choose good investments, and make sure you never have to sell them at a bad time.

It doesn't matter how awesome your investments are, at times they will drop in value. If you're forced to sell investments when they're down, you will lose money. It's that simple.

The key is having enough money to cover all the spending you want or need to do so you need never access investment funds at a bad time.

The key to making sure you have enough cash to cover spending is your spending and saving strategy: your budget.

I talk to a lot of people who are resistant to budgeting. Perhaps they don't want to restrict themselves or they're holding onto some of the budgeting myths I'll bust below, or perhaps they just don't see the need.

This thinking can be seriously costly.

The sooner you lean into your budget and plan around your saving and spending, the sooner you'll get on the Virgin Millionaire fast track.

Budgeting doesn't need to mean pinching pennies or counting every dollar you spend. And it doesn't need to be hard.

Why you need a budget

There are three powerful reasons why you need a budget. It is important to be clear both on where you need to get to and on what you want to do next, and it's important to reduce stress on your money journey. Each reason is compelling in its own right, but the power of the three combined will I hope enable you to rethink your approach to this key area of managing your money.

Your budget tells you where you need to get to

You'll only be truly financially free once you know how much money you want and need, and are confident you have the investments to deliver. This means you must have a working budget.

It might have you spending $1000, $10000 or $100000 a month. But you need the budget numbers to have real confidence you'll get there.

Your budget tells you when you'll get there

Once you know what true money success looks like, and where you want to get to with your money, you need a plan. This will be the centrepiece of your Virgin Millionaire toolkit, something to get in place asap.

The first time you draw up your Virgin Millionaire plan and map out your financial trajectory, you may not be fully on track to achieve full smart money freedom in the timeframe you'd like. This is part of the process. It's only once you know what needs to be done that you can get on with it.

Your budget dictates the progress you'll make towards your end goal, and it's impossible to set up a plan that will work without this budget.

Once you have your long-term plan and the pathway to reach your goal, you can (and should) break it down into smaller chunks. While the best way to manage your plan depends on you and on what's important to you, it's very helpful and borderline necessary to have a clear 12-month target for savings, investments and debt balance, so you're clear on what you're working towards.

Again, it's impossible to do this without a solid budget and a day-to-day process for managing your money.

Your budget tells you what to do next

Most people don't realise how much a budget and a planned savings rate influences what investments make sense for you. Consider this example.

You're at the Foundations stage of your money, and your next big goal is to purchase your first investment property. You've got some money in savings, say $25k, and you know you need $32k for your property deposit.

If you've got a solid budget and you know you're able to consistently save $3000 a month, you'll know you're less than four months away from having your deposit. Given how close you are to having enough to make your property purchase, saving in cash is probably a pretty sensible idea.

If, on the other hand, you're saving $100 a month, it's going to take around six years to save that deposit. Because it's going to take a fair bit of time to build up the cash, you should seriously consider investing your savings to help build the deposit faster.

How much you're saving essentially tells you what money moves make sense for you. But if you aren't clear about your goal, you're playing a guessing game that can be dangerous when it comes to your bigger and more important financial moves.

Saving the deposit for your first investment property is a straightforward example, but investment options will come up throughout your money journey. When they do, having a clear handle on your budget and savings capacity will be a huge help in choosing what will work best for you.

Your budget eliminates stress and pressure

Some people think budgeting is stressful, but the opposite is true. When you have a budget that works, you have all the money you need for spending that's coming up, you're clear on what's left over to save and invest, and you're clear about the next move to make with your money.

The single biggest way people end up under financial pressure and stress is when they don't plan their spending, saving and investing. Without a good plan you're just doing stuff based on what feels right or seems to make sense in the moment. This is unlikely to lead to optimal outcomes. But when you plan and manage your budget well, you can accurately predict how much money you have available for saving and investing, leading to better decisions that are fully aligned with your Virgin Millionaire journey.

Your budget enables you to choose investments consistent with how much money you have available, and to add in a buffer for unexpected or unplanned expenses and emergencies. If you do this well, you should never end up without the money to cover the spending you want or need to do. You also should never be forced to sell investments at the wrong time.

As explained in chapter 4, investing in property is the single biggest lever you can use to accelerate your progress towards smart money freedom.

But any time you buy property, there will almost certainly be a cashflow cost in excess of rental income in the form of mortgage repayments and ongoing property costs.

If you overextend yourself or don't plan and manage risk well, you can get caught short of the money you want or need for the spending that's important to you today. You could be forced to sacrifice things that are important to you, or even have to sell your property. On top of selling costs, you could risk a loss of capital if the market is down. Both scenarios are avoidable.

So long as your budget and saving plans are rock solid, you'll know exactly how much money you can afford to invest in a property purchase without risking lifestyle spending. You can add a buffer to protect you against such risks as rising interest rates or rental vacancy. You'll be able to hold your investment property forever, or at least for as long as it takes for you to get the benefits you're aiming for.

Your budget is the critical factor.

Why you need a pay rise

In the current cost-of-living crisis, with record inflation, rent rises, high petrol prices and rapid increases in interest rates, many people are struggling to make ends meet, let alone finding a way to save.

But most people are missing a trick. I'm going to cover how to budget and how to cut costs. I admit there's a limit to how much you can cut expenses. But there's no limit to how much you can increase your income. Today it's easier than ever to earn more money, but too often people ignore this lever to improve their financial trajectory.

Getting a pay rise is your secret weapon when it comes to saving. If you earn more you can save more without sacrificing anything.

Earning more (read: enough) is a critical part of making your ideal rate of progress on your Virgin Millionaire journey. Not only will you cover spending more comfortably, but you'll be able to save and invest more.

I've worked with a lot of people over the years, and their incomes have ranged from well below the average to over $1 million. Often those at the lower end of the scale are hardworking, switched-on and intelligent, and often they're working just as hard as those who are paid way more.

Your income could be the result of circumstance, industry, personal situation or choices. It is important you enjoy your work, but for most people there are other options for enjoyable, better-paying work that you're either in a position to do already or that you can position yourself to do in the future.

You can certainly become a Virgin Millionaire on a lower income but it's much harder. If creating smart money freedom is important to you, then along with your saving and investment plan you'll need a plan for increasing your employment income. Your aim should be to build your income at least to a level that gives you enough spare cash to hit your saving and investing milestones in a timeframe you're happy with.

I'll now cover ways you can pump up your income and save more without spending a single dollar less today. You don't have to do all (or any) of these. My aim is to introduce the things you *could* do to boost your income.

Get paid more in your current role

There's a talent war on. Good companies are struggling to find (and keep) good people so speak to your boss or employer about what you'd need to do to earn more money in your current role.

A good company knows that more output means better outcomes so it's likely to be open to the conversation. If you can position your role and the work you produce to be more profitable, you deserve to share in the uplift.

Get a promotion

Understanding the next step in your career and accelerating your development to get there sooner means faster income growth. Chat with your employer about what this could look like for you and what you'd need to do to get there.

Taking this path may take a little longer and require a little more effort, but the payoff can be a big salary uplift in the long term. It's common for people to be focused on the day-to-day, but keeping a laser focus on your next big step up will get you there faster.

Change jobs or companies

Annual wage growth is only 4.2 per cent but statistics show the average salary bump when changing jobs to be 14.8 per cent. Based on the average income of $98 218 this means a potential annual pay bump of $14 536 and highlights a huge opportunity to pump up your income. In today's low-unemployment job market, a stack of companies are hiring.

If you're considering this path, do your research and find a company that will be good to work with long term. The last thing you want to do is change jobs only to realise that you hate the role or the company or that they're struggling financially. Do your due diligence and choose wisely.

Get a second job

This will involve more hours at work, but there are always companies looking for part-time or casual workers. Picking up just one extra shift a week can make the difference between struggling to break even and saving enough to get ahead investing.

Technology is making it super simple to pick up gig work. You could drive for a rideshare service, make deliveries or jump on Airtasker. All these options will give you a quick injection of cash to get you to your next money milestone with no long-term obligations or commitments.

Start a side hustle or business

This one shouldn't be taken lightly given how much work is likely to be involved or the potential risks, but if you have a skill set or passion you can monetise you can build a second source of income to supplement your full-time career pay cheque.

Technology is making this easier by the day but a word of warning. It's easy to be lured into the side-hustle life by the promise of easy money only to discover it can come with a huge amount of work for not much money. Do your research before jumping in.

Make your pay rise happen

It's possible to lever your income *without* making any sacrifices at all. Don't ignore the power of a pay rise to accelerate your money success.

There are a lot of different ways to increase your income. Some will be wrong for you but others may suit your skill set, interests and life stage. Take the time to understand your options and think about whether any of these levers might grow your income and accelerate your progress.

Create a smart saving plan (budget)

I'll now explain how to create the last budget you'll ever need. Before we get stuck in, I'll frame it up so you can see the power of the process and why it will seriously impact your progress towards smart money freedom.

The average saving rate in Australia today is currently 3.2 percent. This suggests someone on the average income of $98 218 would be saving $60 a week.

This compares to our peak savings rate of 23.6 per cent just a few years ago. Yes, the world does seem different now, but finding a way to boost your savings by even a small amount will have a huge impact.

If you're 20 today and you were to save at double the current average rate (total $120 weekly) and invest your savings in the share market, your money would grow by an *additional* $2 540 862 by age 65 compared to someone saving at the average rate.

Not saving results in an opportunity cost not just from the amount of money you don't save this week, month or year but from how much your savings would have grown over time.

Saving isn't easy, but when you have a proven process to follow you'll be inspired to save more.

List your income and spending

The first step in creating a savings plan is to list all the spending you need to do and all the spending you want to do. Line this up with your income to see how much, or how little, is left over.

My preference is to use a spreadsheet but if you prefer to do this old school, use or adapt table 6.1 (overleaf). If you want to use some tech, I've set up a free spreadsheet you can download here: bit.ly/virginmillionaire.

Your aim at step one is to get everything down on paper. Think about your spending, including what's discretionary. Don't hold anything back. At this stage you don't need to worry too much about whether your budget is in balance because it probably won't be. The next step is to start prioritising.

Table 6.1 spending and savings planning

Expense	Category	Amount ($)	Frequency
Regular income	Income	1300	weekly
Overtime	Income	150	weekly
Total income		**1450**	**weekly**
Rent	Fixed	500	weekly
Utilities		65	weekly
Subscriptions		40	weekly
Food shopping		320	weekly
Eating out		50	weekly
Holidays		150	weekly
Random		100	weekly
Add new			
Total expenses		**1225**	**weekly**
Net savings		**225**	**weekly**

As you're listing your spending, keep in mind expenses will fit pretty neatly into five distinct categories. Use the categories list to think about your different areas of spending and make sure nothing is missed:

- **Fixed costs:** These are your bills and the boring stuff. They're easy to predict and easy to automate. They are expenses that just need to be paid.

- **Spending:** This is your main day-to-day discretionary spending, including food beyond the basics and entertainment. It's the category that's most commonly responsible for blowing your budget and stalling savings.

- **Debt:** Everyone's least favourite category, but it's important to nail it down.

- **Lifestyle:** This is for your bigger ticket, discretionary expenses like travel, new tech gear, things for your house and other less regular spending like gifts. The spending in this category is likely to be the things that bring you the most enjoyment, so they're important to include in your plan to ensure it's sustainable over the long term.

- **Saving and investing:** When you work through your budget, your saving and investing can look like what's left over, but it's obviously far from the least important item in your budget.

Pro tip: When you're going through this process, don't worry so much about how much you spent in the past. What matters is how much you want to spend in the future. When you're putting together a budget, particularly if you're doing it for the first time or for the first time in a while, it's likely you're looking to make significant changes in spending.

Reduce spending to save more

Please don't shoot the messenger, but the next stage involves cutting out things that are less important to you so you can save more. You shouldn't need to cut out anything that's truly important to you.

Important spending should be prioritised so you can make it happen. Focus on cutting down on things you don't value as much. Everyone is as unique as a snowflake and your priorities are likely to be different from those of most other people. What that means is that, once again, there is no right way to do this. There's only *the way that's right for you*.

The right way for you means you will have the money to spend on the things that really matter, allowing enough money to save and invest at a rate that allows you to make the progress you want. If you're struggling to make this happen, revisit the section on why you need a pay rise.

Clearly your spending needs to be balanced against your income. If you're on a low income and have a lot of spending that's really important, you will need to have a plan to increase your income. The power is in your hands.

Fixed expenses

There are two quick and easy ways to reduce your fixed costs: cutting spending and shopping around.

Compare the costs of insurances and utilities. When every dollar counts, a small amount of time invested regularly will ensure you're getting the sharpest deals and not spending more than you need to.

Another way to save more on fixed expenses is potentially a slower burn but has an even greater impact. Be mindful how you add in fixed costs over time and cut out those that are less important to you.

It's estimated that 17 per cent of Aussies forget to cancel unused subscriptions, which can cost hundreds of dollars a year. Eliminating fixed costs you don't want or need will move the dial on your savings.

It's easy for such costs to accumulate. You hire a cleaner, a dog walker, a personal trainer. If you do this without thinking about the impact over time, it's easy to rack up extra fixed costs that can wreck your savings capacity.

Many of these services are hard to cut once you get used to having them in your life. Any of them can be on your 'important' list, and there are a few that I value highly and include in my own spending. The key to success here is that these things should be included only when you can comfortably afford them and still save and invest at the rate you want.

As you move forward and progress through the Smart Money Stages, think before adding in expenses that could compromise your savings progress. And if you've already accumulated these kinds of expenses, reconsider their importance.

Spending

In addition to entertainment and clothes, this category includes all your spending on food and medical costs, two areas that are necessary to live. It's easy to spend a lot here, but if you plan well you can keep your costs low, and it will go a long way to boosting your savings.

How much money you allocate to this category is going to be a big driver of your day-to-day lifestyle and your savings. Include what's important and ruthlessly cut what's not.

Depositing savings in a separate bank account each week will help ensure you hit your savings targets.

Debt

Bad debt drains your cashflow and your savings capacity along with it. Trying to get ahead with your money while running bad debt is like pouring water into a leaky bucket.

A key step on your journey to saving success is to eliminate bad debt from your life so you are not dealing with dead interest costs or the costs to your cashflow of repayment. Getting rid of debt can take time and work, but it's essential if you're to get to where you really want to be. If you need help, you can access some free training here: bit.ly/virginmillionaire.

When it comes to good debt, compare providers regularly to cut interest costs. The market for mortgages is highly competitive and it's easy to save a heap by shopping around.

Lifestyle expenses

Lifestyle spending drives the most satisfaction and enjoyment and for that reason it's an important spending category when it comes to ensuring your spending plan is sustainable for the long term.

But you can cut back lifestyle spending in the short term if needed to allow your other spending and savings goals to work. Planning ahead will also help you spend less.

Pro tip: Unexpected expenses are the main reason most people can't stick to their savings goals — things like having to replace your phone or laptop, home repairs, or a string of personal or family events that arise unexpectedly.

To prevent unforeseen costs from throwing out your spending and saving plan, recognise they're inevitable and allow for them. If the money you set aside isn't needed, you can always reallocate it to savings.

Systemise your savings

Once you've followed through the steps above, you should have a solid savings plan that allows you to spend on what matters most to you and still be able to save at a rate you're happy with.

But a plan on its own will *not* deliver the results you want.

Even if you are one of the few people who can resist the immediate pleasures of spending and are naturally good at saving, having an automated system in place will make your day-to-day money management, and your life, easier.

When I talk about systemising your savings, I mean having a different bank account for each bucket of money. You'll set up a system to ensure bills and debt will be paid automatically without your having to stress about whether there's enough put aside. You will be clear on your pocket money (spending), your lifestyle fund will be building and your savings and investments will be quarantined and growing. Your confidence in your system will keep you motivated.

If you use the savings planner tool, you can use the spreadsheet to categorise your spending and tell you exactly how much to transfer to each of your accounts and when. If you're running this yourself, the key is to designate every expense into its category then automate in line with the banking system outlined in figure 6.1.

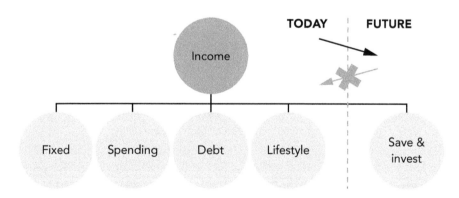

Figure 6.1 the Pivot automated saving system

In my completely biased opinion, the system we've created is a solid starting point. Of course you can modify it to suit. At the end of the day your job is to organise your spending and saving so the system is straightforward and works for you.

Do be aware that when it comes to saving you will face unconscious resistance as your inner spender resists being tamed.

In the worst case, you will self-sabotage. You will look for excuses for why the saving and investment approach you've planned won't or can't work, or at least not right now. Just as there's always a reason to delay exercising more, eating healthier or drinking less. But it will work if you are committed to reaching your goal. Shutting down that negative inner voice will accelerate your results, and using a system thousands of others have found to work will reduce the number of excuses you can make for why you can't hit your savings target.

Smart Money Stages and saving

Saving money is the lead domino that drives every investment decision you make on the path to becoming a Virgin Millionaire. I can't overstate the importance of nailing this crucial area of your money. But you should be aware that what's required will depend on which Smart Money Stage you're at (see table 6.2).

Table 6.2 Smart Money Stages and saving

Success outcomes	Foundations	Focus	Optimise	Accelerate	Impact
Saving	Saving consistently each month in line with your plan, with only minor deviations.	Saving and spending well and consistently.	9/10 satisfaction with saving and spending.	10/10 satisfaction with saving and spending—ideal lifestyle spending fully achieved.	Ideal lifestyle spending with surplus savings.

Saving: Foundations

At the Foundations stage you're trying to build early traction and momentum, so having tight control of your spending will help you progress faster and kick-start your Virgin Millionaire momentum.

Focus on building good habits around your spending behaviour, as they will make your life a whole lot easier at each of the stages that follow.

Look to pare back any spending you don't feel is crucial so you can save more, and focus on how you can increase your income.

Short-term income boosts will help you hit the targets that will enable you to enter the next stage, but given you still have a way to go on your Virgin Millionaire journey, you should also be thinking longer term. Often the longer-term shifts in your income will be larger and have a greater impact, whether you decide to further your education, set yourself up for promotion and career progression, or switch industries or careers.

Saving: Focus

At the Focus stage your biggest saving and investment goal is to purchase your first investment property and the more you can save the faster you'll get there. Following on from the Foundations stage, you should maintain strict control over your spending to keep savings strong.

If you cut out things at the Foundations stage that are important to you, you might consider reintroducing them now, so long as you can do so without seriously compromising your progress.

At this stage increasing your income should still be on your radar so you can increase savings and accelerate progress.

Saving: Optimise

Once you land at the Optimise stage, you will have put in the work to create momentum and consistency around saving and investing. It's important to keep the momentum building, but you can start to think about finding more balance between saving and spending.

If there are things important to you from a lifestyle perspective, give this some attention now. By this point you will have solid investments in both shares and property that are building and growing for you, which should relieve some of the early pressure on your savings rate.

As you work through this stage, you will likely increase your spending until it is closer to your planned ideal lifestyle spending. Increasing your spending should feel good, but in terms of smart money freedom there are a few downsides to keep in mind.

First, spending will slow your rate of savings. Second, it will increase your smart money freedom target number because you now need to support a higher level of spending in the future, so you will need more money in investments to achieve this higher income. While these are negatives in terms of your financial progress, they are positives in terms of your lifestyle. Balance is key here.

In terms of smart money freedom it's important to be happy with the journey as well as the destination. Moving towards your ideal lifestyle spending is an important element of this. But keep in mind that the more you spend now, the more work you'll need to do in the future and that at the next stages more and more will be possible.

At this point you need to restrict yourself less, but remaining clear and confident about how much money you need for spending and savings is critical. It's highly likely that at this stage you'll be running a significant amount of good tax-deductible debt, and will likely be considering adding more good debt for further investments.

For your leveraged investing to work, for your risk to be managed and for you to have confidence and eliminate stress while you're pushing hard on investing, you will want to be in complete control of your savings and spending. Don't fall into the trap of thinking that, because you have more money to spend, having a good saving system isn't as important here as it was in the past.

Saving: Accelerate

At this stage you should be able to comfortably cover everything that's important to you. As at the previous stage, as you increase your spending to cover your ideal lifestyle, you will increase your targets at the same time as you slow down your rate of saving.

By the time you graduate from the Accelerate stage, you should be at a 10/10 satisfaction level with your spending and your saving rate. But you will still need to think carefully about what your ideal lifestyle looks like and how much money you'll need to fund it. You're getting closer and closer to smart money freedom and the last thing you want is to realise you've missed something and have to go back a step.

As at the Optimise stage, the risk here is that you'll start running fast and loose with your controls around spending and saving and lose clarity. This would be a costly mistake.

Saving: Impact

At this point you should already be at your ideal level of spending and be able to do pretty much whatever you want. This might include tapping out from regular structured employment for a pay cheque.

But keep in mind that once you turn off your income tap you won't be adding to your investments at the rate you have been, which will make keeping on top of your spending and saving even more crucial than at any other stage.

The good news is that you will have built some serious skills and good habits around your planning, spending and saving, so your focus will be on maintaining what you've achieved rather than starting something new.

THE WRAP

The many myths around budgeting and most people's natural tendency to spend rather than save can make for a dangerous combination. At best, progress falls short and at worst saving and investing slow or cease. Both scenarios are avoidable.

Most people find strategies for investing, wealth building and tax saving more exciting than those for budgeting and saving. But it's your budget that dictates which of the more exciting options make sense, so it needs to be a first step.

In my experience of helping tens of thousands of people with their money, savings is an area that is truly nailed by fewer than 1 per cent of the population. The other 99 per cent must struggle so much harder to achieve their financial potential.

I want you to be a savings superstar. I want you to get it and start the habit-building that's needed around your spending and savings to drive the progress you want and deserve on your Virgin Millionaire journey.

Take action

- Set your mind firmly on the fact that budgeting is important regardless of how big your income is or which Smart Money Stage you've reached.

- Understand the three big benefits of budgeting: clarity on where you need to get to, what to do next, and elimination of financial stress.

- Consider what you can do to increase your income, and ensure that growing your employment income is part of your financial focus.

- Map out your budget to include all your current spending and income.

- Prioritise your spending ruthlessly to increase your savings. You can use our template at bit.ly/virginmillionaire.

- Create an automated savings system to support your saving and spending plan.

- Set a timeline to check in on your savings progress and build your budgeting muscle.

CHAPTER 7

Tax strategies

A while back I started working with a young couple I'll call Amanda and Adam. They had one child and were planning bub number two in the next couple of years, and they had some big financial goals for their future.

Amanda worked in sales and Adam was a marketing executive. They were making a solid combined household income of $280000 and saving at a rate of $3000 a month, investing around $2000 in ETFs and putting the remaining $1000 into their high-interest savings account.

As is the case with many couples, one was more involved in managing the household finances. For these guys it was Amanda, whose dad was big on investing and had got her interested when she was very young. She had done well and Amanda and Adam were pretty stoked that they had built up a portfolio of almost $200000 in ETFs.

The challenge came as they started settling down and growing their family. They were keen to get into the property market but with Sydney property prices, finding a place in the area they wanted to live that was big enough seemed almost impossible. Even with the money they had in savings and investments, they felt they didn't have enough income to cover mortgage payments and live the lifestyle they wanted.

As they planned for their second child, they looked at the financial costs. Maternity leave and a reduction in income for Amanda, together with the costs of actually having a child, would be followed by a second set of daycare expenses. Amanda and Adam felt these financial hurdles would slow down their ability to get into the property market.

And property prices were continuing to rise. They worried that the longer they waited to buy their first property, the less they'd be able to afford and the further they'd be from their ultimate financial goals.

They came to me to figure out how to make the most of the money they had and what they could do to move ahead faster.

We realised there were a couple of easy wins. They continued to save and invest at the same rate but they tweaked how they were doing that in order to create a total tax saving of over $40 000. This enabled them to buy their first property 18 months earlier than they'd thought they would be able to. And it gets even better.

In the 18 months after their purchase, the property's value increased by over $135 000. This, combined with a tax saving of over $40 000, meant they made an extra $175 000.

We could stop there, but to understand the real benefit it's necessary to look at how this $175 000 would grow in the future. Amanda and Adam purchased the property and received the benefit when Amanda was 36, so even based on a conservative growth rate of 6.5 per cent, compounding would grow that money to $1 146 764 by the time she was 65.

Not a bad outcome for making a few small tweaks and using the tax rules a little bit smarter. This shows the power of tax planning.

I've already discussed the different levers you can use to shift and improve your financial trajectory: spend less, save more, earn more, work for longer, use more debt, take on more risk and save on tax.

Saving on tax is my favourite of these levers because it's the only one that doesn't require increased risk, sacrifice or working harder or longer.

When you're smarter with your tax, you use the existing rules to your advantage to make money from the money you already have. If you're serious about being a Virgin Millionaire, tax planning is something you need to get right.

The tax rules are confusing and complicated and can be overwhelming. To make things worse, your tax position doesn't always become clear until you've completed your return.

As a result, tax often goes into the too hard basket. It's put off for a tomorrow that never comes while you miss out on the opportunity to get your money working smarter and harder.

The Australian tax system

In Australia we work under a marginal tax-rate system, also known as a progressive tax system. The current marginal tax brackets (including full Medicare levy) are shown in table 7.1.

Table 7.1 Australian marginal tax brackets and rates

Taxable income	Tax on this income
0–$18 200	Nil
$18 201–$45 000	18% for each $1 over $18 200*
$45 001–$135 000	32% for each $1 over $45 000 (plus tax from previous bracket)
$135 001–$190 000	39% for each $1 over $135 000 (plus tax from previous brackets)
$190 001 and over	47% for each $1 over $190 000 (plus tax from previous brackets)

*Medicare levy of 2% commences at $29 033.

How tax deductions work

As your income increases, so does your marginal tax rate. The higher rates only apply to income earned above each threshold number so even if your income is well into the top marginal tax bracket of $190 000+, you still pay no tax on the first $18 200.

So if you're earning a salary and then start investing in your own name, any investment income will be added to your salary income and be taxed at your marginal rate. As this income grows, it may even push you into the next tax bracket and further increase your tax rate.

In some ways this is a good thing, because it means that your investment income is increasing. But because marginal tax rates increase as your income increases, it means that the more investment income you earn (or plan to earn) the more tax you will pay.

Tax deductions work by reducing your taxable income, which reduces the amount of tax you will pay. It's worth noting that when you claim a tax deduction, you will only ever get a percentage of the deduction back in tax.

It works like this. If you're currently in the top marginal tax bracket of 47 per cent and you earn an extra $1000 in income, that full $1000 will be added to your taxable income and be taxed at your marginal rate of 47 per cent. The tax will be $470.

On the other hand, a $1000 tax deduction reduces your taxable income by $1000, which means you will receive a refund at your marginal rate of 47 per cent and pay $470 less in that tax year.

The more you earn and the higher your marginal tax rate, the more benefit every dollar of tax deductions will be to you. This means the more you earn, the more valuable it is to maximise your deductions.

You only get one tax rate

A common tax myth holds that there are different taxes for different types of income, but this just isn't true.

Every income earner has just one taxable income, and just one tax scale applies to that income. The ATO adds together all your income from all sources, including your salary, overtime, bonuses, commission, interest from bank accounts, dividends from shares and rental income from investment properties. This is your 'assessable income'.

Tax deductions are added together to determine your total deductions. These are subtracted from your assessable income to determine your net assessable income. This is the figure the ATO uses to establish how much tax you will pay.

For salaried employees, your employer withholds a certain amount of your income to cover your estimated tax.

Note that when you invest no one withholds the tax. As I will go on to discuss, you're responsible for any tax consequences.

When you complete a tax return, the ATO calculates the amount of your total tax payable. You then take away any withheld tax to establish how much you'll receive as a refund or, if your tax bill is more than the amount withheld, you'll receive a tax bill.

This was an issue for Amanda and Adam, and one of the quick wins we used to save them over $1000 a year in tax. They had an investment portfolio of $200 000 generating investment income of around $10 000 a year. The portfolio was in Amanda's name and because she was earning at the top marginal rate of 47 per cent, the tax on the investment income was $4700 a year.

Adam was on a lower tax rate of 34 per cent (this was before the 2024 tax rate changes), so we shifted their investments into his name. He was taxed $3450 a year, an immediate saving of over $1000. This saving would grow each year as Amanda and Adam's investment balance and investment income grew. With the new tax cuts that have come in since we set things up, Adam's tax rate has dropped to 32 per cent, so the annual saving is now more than $1500.

Long-term capital gains tax discount

The goal of pretty much every investment is that when you sell it, you'll get more than you paid so you'll make a gain. In investing and tax jargon, this is referred to as a capital gain because the value of your capital has increased.

Increasing your capital is a good thing but there is a small downside in that investment gains, like any other capital gains, are taxable. They are added to your other assessable income and taxed at your marginal rate.

However, because the government wants to encourage longer-term investment, the ATO offers a tax break. If you've held your investment for 12 months or more, you can reduce your capital gain by 50 per cent and pay tax on only half the gain.

For example, if you buy a property for $500000 and then sell it for $600000, your gain will be $100000. If you've owned that property for less than 12 months, the full $100000 will be added to your assessable income and taxed at your marginal rate. But if you've held the investment for longer than 12 months, the taxable capital gain will be reduced by 50 per cent to $50000. This discounted gain is added to your assessable income and taxed at your marginal rate.

This discount has the potential to drive some significant tax savings and ties into some of the tax strategies and structures I'll explain in this and the next chapter.

Top tax-saving strategies

Tax planning can help you build the money you already have. I'll now unpack the most effective, and legal, tax-reduction strategies you can use to cut your tax bill and hold onto more of your hard-earned money.

Keep good records

To be good at tax, you need to be organised with your admin. It's probably the single most important thing you can do when it comes to saving tax.

It's simple but simple doesn't mean easy. Many people miss out on deductions because they don't keep good records throughout the year and have to scramble to find what they can at tax time.

You have two objectives when it comes to keeping your tax records.

First, keep everything organised in one place so it's easy to put in your tax claim.

Second, keep a longer-term record of your deductions and returns in case you're audited in the future.

Throughout the year I track my deductions on a spreadsheet and I save everything tax-related in a folder on my computer. At the end of the year I ship it all to my accountant.

Technology is making it easier to track and manage your tax, and every year there are new apps to choose from. If you find one that works for you, great. If you're old school and prefer hard copies in a shoebox or folder, go for it. The important thing is you're making it easy both to do your return and to keep a clear audit trail.

At the end of the day, the taxation system isn't going away, so creating a system that works for you now and will work into the future will save you time and money.

Maximise your deductions

No matter what you do for work or how you do it, you're likely to be able to claim expenses. Whether it's work-related equipment, travel costs, home-office expenses or any of the weird and wonderful things in between, you need to understand what's deductible if you're to take full advantage of the rules.

The ATO has a heap of helpful guides and content on their website that show what you can claim and what you can't. As you move through each tax year, you'll become familiar with what you need to track and record to make claiming easy at tax time.

A word of warning. Because you only get part of any tax-deductible cost refunded, spending money on something you don't need just to get a deduction doesn't make financial sense.

Prepay expenses before EOFY

If it's getting towards the end of the financial year and you have tax-deductible expenses planned for the near future, you can benefit from bringing them forward into the current financial year.

For example, you may be planning to buy a heap of new office equipment in July. If you do this spending in June instead, you'll be able to claim the tax deductions and get the tax benefit a full year earlier. Because the money is in your bank account you can put it to work for you.

Common expenses to bring forward are work-related spending and financial and tax advice costs. It's even possible to bring forward interest payments on tax-deductible investment debt. Again, given you only receive as a tax benefit part of any amount spent, this only makes financial sense if you were going to incur the expense anyway.

Negative gearing

This is one of my favourite tax strategies as it combines two powerful benefits in one strategy: tax deductions and the power of leverage or gearing.

Negative gearing works when you borrow money to invest and the costs of your investment, including interest on investment debt, are more than the income.

The most common form of negative gearing in Australia is buying an investment property. When you borrow from the bank to buy an investment property, your costs include mortgage repayments and the costs of operating the property—strata fees, insurance, maintenance. At the same time, you receive an income from your property investment in the form of rental income.

Negative gearing refers to an investment's negative overall cashflow. For example, if borrowing + ongoing costs are more than the rental income, the overall cashflow is negative. You will need to fund the shortfall from your other income. If the income is more than all the expenses, the cashflow is positive and this is termed positive gearing.

Note that the reason you'd choose an investment with a negative cash flow is because your total return includes the long-term growth in the property's value, which typically will be much higher than the shorter-term out-of-pocket costs. Refer back to chapters 2 and 3 on leverage and property if you need a refresher.

The tax-saving power of negative gearing from claiming any shortfall means you pay less tax, which covers a large chunk of the cost of running your investment. If your taxable income is above $45 000 a year, your marginal tax rate will be at least 32 per cent; if it's above $135 000 your tax rate will be 39 per cent, and if your income is above $190 000 your tax rate will be 47 per cent.

This means you will be reimbursed between 32 per cent and 47 per cent of any costs when you file your tax return. For example, if the out-of-pocket expenses of running your investment property were $10 000 a year, the ATO would refund you the tax paid on this $10 000, between $3200 and $4700 (based on your tax rate), reducing your investment costs to between $5300 and $6800 a year.

You can use the money saved in tax each year to further build your investment portfolio.

It's worth noting when it comes to negative gearing and property that you can't claim a tax deduction for principal repayments on a mortgage. This is because principal is a capital cost rather than an expense.

At the same time, given that the full value of every single dollar you pay against the principal of your loan reduces your debt and therefore increases your asset/wealth position, this is actually better than just being able to claim it as a tax deduction.

To sum up, negative gearing can be a serious accelerator but never invest for tax benefits alone. All your investments, particularly those that entail borrowing, need to be solid before the tax benefits. Any reduction in tax should only ever be the cream on top.

Negative gearing was another strategy we leveraged for Amanda and Adam. When we met they were considering buying a property as their own home but they realised buying an investment property instead would deliver two significant benefits.

The first was the almost $20000 in annual tax savings. But the second was even more powerful. They didn't need a property that would accommodate their growing family. Instead they could choose a rock-solid but more affordable property sooner.

They did in fact move into the property in the short term to access the first home buyer benefits discussed in chapter 3. but from the outset they planned to move out and run the property as an investment into the future.

Debt recycling

This is one of my favourite strategies for homeowners with non-tax-deductible home-loan debt because it allows you to convert it into tax-deductible investment debt.

As at the end of 2023, the Australian Bureau of Statistics (ABS) showed the average owner-occupier mortgage size to be $584907, and at the time of writing in February 2024 the average variable mortgage interest rate is 7.26 per cent.

If you have an average-sized mortgage sitting at the average variable interest rate, using debt recycling would generate annual tax deductions of $42464. In turn, this would create tens of thousands of dollars in tax savings, all of which you could use to get ahead.

With a debt recycling strategy, you make extra payments on your non-tax-deductible home-loan debt, and at the same time draw the same amount from debt. This money is then used to invest, typically into share-type investments like funds or ETFs. Because the purpose of this new borrowing is investment, the interest on this portion of the debt is tax-deductible.

When you follow a debt recycling strategy over time, your non-deductible home-loan debt is converted or recycled into tax-deductible investment debt. In the example in table 7.2, you have an average-sized mortgage of $584907 against a property valued at $1 million, and have a spare $500 per week you want to use to save or invest.

In week one of the strategy, you pay your spare $500 as an extra payment on your mortgage. At the same time you withdraw $500 from the new loan set up for investment purposes, and invest this money in a share portfolio.

Table 7.2 how debt recycling works in practice, day 0 to year 10

	Day 0	Day 7	Day 365	Day 3650 (year 10 of strategy)
Total home (non-deductible) debt	$584907	$584407	$532907	$344907
Total investment (deductible) debt	$0	$500	$26000	$260000
Total debt	$584907	$584907	$584907	$584907

Note that because this strategy revolves around paying down non-tax-deductible mortgage debt, it's viable only for people who have a mortgage against their home or another property that's not an investment.

In table 7.3 I've built on our previous example to show the interest deductions that result and the tax you can save. I've used a marginal tax rate of 32 per cent, the rate paid on an annual taxable income of above $45 000.

Table 7.3 how debt recycling works in practice over the long term

	At end of year 1	At end of year 10	At end of year 25
Total home (non-deductible) debt	$558 907	$324 907	$0
(Non-deductible) interest @ 7.26%	$38 689	$23 588	$0
Total investment (deductible) debt	$26 000	$260 000	$584 907
(Deductible) interest @ 7.26%	$1887 p.a.	$18 876 p.a.	$42 464 p.a.
Tax refund @ 32%	$566 p.a.	$5663 p.a.	$13 588 p.a.
Total debt	$584 907	$584 907	$584 907

The tax savings over the long term are significant at $13 588 every year. That's just for paying down your mortgage at the same time as you invest. This money can be used to invest more and get ahead faster, or you can choose to spend it now.

Another benefit of this strategy is that because the long-term return on shares of 9.8 per cent is higher than the long-term average mortgage interest rate, your share portfolio will grow faster than the interest you pay on your investment debt. Eventually when you sell your shares, you should have enough to clear your investment debt and have money left over.

If you're considering debt recycling as a strategy, you should note there are different ways to structure your mortgage debt and some are better than others. Given the value in getting this strategy right, along with the complexity of actually executing the strategy, my strong suggestion is that you get good advice.

Ideally you should put in place a solid financial plan, but at the very least get the support of an experienced mortgage broker who knows their stuff when it comes to this specific strategy. Getting this wrong can be seriously costly, not to mention frustrating, so investing a bit of time and some money will be worth it.

If you're investing and have a mortgage, you might choose to invest the money directly into your investment account, which is to say not through a debt facility as part of a debt recycling strategy and forgo the tax deductions. Or you could choose to follow the same investing structure but structure it in a smarter way and cut your tax bill in the process.

There are very few no brainers when it comes to your money, but if you're a homeowner looking to both pay down your mortgage and invest, this is one of them.

Any time you borrow money to invest there are risks you need to consider and manage carefully, but one of the best things about debt recycling is that your total debt levels do not increase at any point. This is because you're consistently reducing one type of debt as you increase another. Your total debt is unchanged. This goes a long way to reducing your risk levels.

Throughout this book I've emphasised the value of choosing rock-solid investments. The benefits of debt recycling will be significantly reduced if you choose average or bad investments. Refer back to chapter 4 for a refresher on how to choose rock-solid investments.

Share investing and franking credits

As discussed in chapter 4, when you buy a stock or share you own a small portion of a company and are entitled to the same portion of that company's profits and growth. When profits are paid out to shareholders they come in the form of a dividend.

In Australia, dividends are often paid from after-tax profits. The company earns a profit, pays tax on that profit and pays out dividends from this money after company tax has been paid.

Because this company's profit income has already been taxed the ATO, in their benevolence, don't tax it again. A tax credit is attached to your dividend that reflects the company tax paid. This tax credit is referred to as a franking credit, and when dividends are paid with franking credits attached they're referred to as franked dividends.

In Australia, the company tax rate is around 30 per cent depending on the size of the company and because personal marginal tax rates are a maximum of 47 per cent of income, in most cases you won't pay much extra tax, if any, on franked dividend income.

These tax credits will seriously move the dial in terms of how much you need to have in investments to deliver your ideal level of after-tax income. Consider this example.

In Australia, the average before-tax income is $98 218. Based on current tax rates, this income attracts $22 218 in tax, leaving you with an after-tax income of $76 000.

Let's imagine this is your ideal level of income. I'm not saying it is, but my example applies regardless of your income target.

If you were aiming to achieve this level of income through investments and your investments didn't pay franked dividends, you'd need to replace the full income, then pay tax, to realise $76 000 in after-tax income.

Using the 5 per cent rule discussed in chapter 1, you'd need around $1 964 360 in investments to achieve this level of income.

If, on the other hand, your investments paid out in franked dividends that were taxed at the company rate of 30 per cent, using the same 5 per cent rule, investments of $1 375 060 would yield the same after-tax income.

For the maths nerds and detail-focused people, here's how it works:

> Franking credit
> = [dividend amount / (1 – company tax rate)] dividend amount

Or:

$$\text{Franking credit } [\$29\,466]$$
$$= [\text{dividend amount} (\$68\,753) / [1 - \text{company tax rate} (30\%)]$$
$$- \text{dividend amount} (\$68\,753)]$$

This shows you can have $589\,300 less in your investment portfolio and earn the same income. You're just as 'wealthy' but with less wealth. This shows the power of smart tax planning.

I will just mention here that this is a simple example and there are a lot of factors to consider when it comes to setting up the best investment portfolio for you. Tax is one of them, but diversification is also very important. Given the Australian share market is small compared to the total global share market, having all of your investments sitting in Australian shares comes with some risks.

But the example *does* show the power of tax planning when you invest.

Superannuation contributions

Under the current rules in Australia, you can contribute up to $30\,000 each year in tax-deductible contributions (also called concessional contributions) to your super fund. This doesn't include money contributed by your employer under the compulsory superannuation guarantee rules, but for most people this leaves room for some significant deductions and, in turn, significant tax savings.

There are two big tax benefits of contributing money to your superannuation fund. First, any deductible contributions to your super fund are taxed at a rate of 15 per cent rather than at personal marginal tax rates.

For example, if you were on an annual income of $100\,000 you'd receive compulsory super contributions of $11\,500 each year (based on the current compulsory super contribution rate of 11.5 per cent). Based on the deductible contribution limit of $30\,000, you would be able to make further deductible contributions to your super fund of up to $18\,500 every year.

If you were to make an extra super contribution of $18 500, you could claim a tax deduction for this full amount. Instead of paying $5920 annual tax at your personal marginal tax rate + Medicare levy of 32 per cent (based on an income of $100 000), you'd pay $2775 based on the super tax rate of 15 per cent. You'd save $3145 in tax, and in turn would end up with an *extra* $3145 in investments working and compounding for you.

It gets even better.

Once money is inside your super fund, the maximum rate of tax you pay on its investment earnings is also 15 per cent, again much lower than the personal marginal tax rates that would apply if the money was invested in your personal name not under your super fund. Based on the long-term share market return of 9.8 per cent and the 15 per cent super tax rate, your after-tax super investment return would be 8.33 per cent [9.8% × (1−15%)].

This rate is significantly higher than your after-tax investment return for non-super investments for which, if your income was above $45 000 with a 32 per cent tax rate, your after-tax investment return would be at most 6.64 per cent [9.8% × (1−32%)], and lower if your tax rate was higher.

So you benefit from tax savings when the money goes into your super fund, and then every year into the future that the money remains invested.

Table 7.4 shows how much your super balance would grow if you were 30 years old and earning the average income with a $50 000 super starting balance and added just $5 a day in extra deductible contributions.

Table 7.4 the impact of $5 daily super contributions over time

Year	5	10	15	20	25	30
Super @ 8.33%	$132 419	$257 240	$446 276	$732 565	$1 166 138	$1 822 770
Contributing +$5 a day	$141 980	$281 279	$492 244	$811 741	$1 295 609	$2 028 408
Difference	$9561	$24 039	$45 968	$79 176	$129 471	$205 638

Even small contributions can make a huge difference over time. If you were to put in more than $5 a day, the benefits would escalate — and quickly.

Under the current rules, once you put money into your super fund it's going to be stuck there until you can access it at age 60. This means that maxing out your super contributions is unlikely to be the first investing strategy you put in place, but given how compelling the tax benefits are it shouldn't be the last.

The right move for you here once again depends on which stage you're at with your money.

First Home Super Saver Scheme

The First Home Super Saver Scheme (or FHSS) is a strategy the Federal Government created to help first-home buyers enter the property market sooner. The strategy allows you to save up to $50000 per person through your super fund by means of tax-deductible concessional contributions, which you can withdraw to use towards your first property purchase. This means for couples the total amount you can use is $100000, which is likely to be most, if not all, your deposit.

Because concessional super contributions attract a tax deduction on the way into your super fund, they reduce your personal tax payable, meaning you can save more money faster than you can by saving outside superannuation.

The rules are a little complex, so if you're thinking about this strategy I strongly suggest you seek advice before getting started. But there are some serious tax savings up for grabs.

The short version is that when you make extra contributions to your super fund, you benefit from a tax deduction at your marginal tax rate, but your super fund pays tax on the contributions at the standard rate of 15 per cent. When the funds are withdrawn from super, they're taxed at your marginal tax rate with a 30 per cent tax offset. This means that for most people the tax benefit will be 15 per cent.

For example, if your tax rate + Medicare levy is 32 per cent on the way into super, the benefit to you is 17 per cent (32 per cent – 15 per cent). When you withdraw the money, it's taxed at your marginal tax rate with the 30 per cent

(*continued*)

offset (32 per cent – 30 per cent). So the total benefit less total cost is 15 per cent (17 per cent – 2 per cent).

But the tax benefits can be lower or higher if your tax rate is different when you make the contributions and when you withdraw the money. This is a big risk for Virgin Millionaires because your income is likely to increase in the future. If you jump up into the next tax bracket while this strategy is in play, the tax benefits will be eroded and in extreme cases you could even be worse off.

On the flip side, if your tax rate reduces, for example when you're taking maternity leave or during any period when your income is lower, the tax benefits can be amplified.

Concessional super contributions combined with the FHSS was another strategy we used with Amanda and Adam that created a tax saving of over $20 000, which helped push them over the line and get their first property sooner.

These guys hit the sweet spot on this strategy because they made their super contributions when Amanda was paying tax at the top marginal rate and withdrew them when her income and tax rate were lower.

We worked hard on their plan and timeline and structured things so they purchased their property just after Amanda returned to work after the birth of their second child. This meant the tax benefit from implementing her FHSS contribution of $50 000 was $14 000. With the $7500 allocated to Adam, their total benefit was $21 500. This extra money was one of the key accelerators that allowed them to buy their first property 18 months sooner than would have been possible otherwise.

Pay for good advice

I've saved the best for last here, because under the Australian tax rules you can claim a tax deduction for the cost of ongoing advice that helps you save tax and generate ongoing investment income.

This means you can get the best professional advice and support to help you navigate your tax and investment planning and effectively get a discount of up to 47 per cent. In this chapter and through this book, my aim is to simplify as much as possible the things you should know and consider when planning to get the most out of the money you have. But the reality is, it's complicated.

While the strategies themselves can be a little tricky, the really tricky thing about your tax and investment planning is to make the right moves at the right time, taking into account both where you are today and your evolving situation.

As things change, the suitability of a strategy or tactic can change. Unless you are aware of this and map the variables into your plan, it can be difficult to make the decisions that are best for you.

This is another point at which you might consider professional advice from someone who's seen it all before and knows what to look out for, the right questions to ask and the best ways to stress test your plan. A good professional is also likely to suggest ideas you may not have considered to help you get more from the money you have today.

Good advice will make you more money than it will cost you, and it's tax-deductible.

Smart Money Stages and tax strategies

The right tax moves and tactics for you today depend on which of the five Smart Money Stages you've reached. Table 7.5 (overleaf) plants some seeds of the things you should be thinking about growing at each stage.

Table 7.5 Smart Money Stages and tax strategies

Success outcomes	Foundations	Focus	Optimise	Accelerate	Impact
Tax	Leverage at least one strategy to save a minimum $1000 p.a. in tax.	Leverage multiple tax strategies to save a minimum $10k p.a. in tax.	Investment strategy to include at least one tax structure outside of superannuation, e.g. bonds, trust, company etc.	Be 100% confident you're not paying more than your fair share in tax.	Multiple tax saving structures in place.

Tax strategies: Foundations

At the Foundations stage your goal is to start building your tax muscle. You'll learn to understand the tax rules and how to use them to your advantage. Your goal for this stage is to use at least one strategy to save a minimum of $1000 each year in tax.

The first thing to focus on is keeping good records. You will set up a system around how you track and manage your tax that will serve you today and into the years ahead. Ensure you're tracking your deductible expenses and keeping good records to make your tax planning and tax returns easier, and to ensure you claim every dollar you can at tax time.

Maximising your deductions and end-of-financial-year prepayments are next up. It's important to remember that tax-deductible expenses still cost you money; they just cost you less because you get the tax back. You should never incur unnecessary expenses just to get the deduction.

Consider deductible super contributions at the Foundations stage, given the immediate tax deduction and the compounding impact of having more money in the lower tax superannuation environment. But until you have purchased your first investment property, my view is that the bulk of your spare cash should be working towards this goal.

That said, starting additional super contributions of small amounts, even $10 a week or month, will help you create a habit you can build on into the future. The added benefit of doing this is that no matter how small your extra super contributions are, once you start making them you'll start paying attention to your super fund.

The great thing about deductible super contributions is that you can have your employer make these automatically from your pre-tax income, meaning you won't feel the full cost.

Another tax strategy you can look at once you start your regular investment plan at the Foundations stage is franked dividend share investing. Given you're likely to be investing smaller amounts at this stage, the dollar benefits are unlikely to be earth-shattering, but understanding the strategy and having something bubbling away will deliver compounding benefits in the long run.

Tax strategies: Focus

By the end of the Focus stage your aim will be to leverage multiple tax strategies to save at least $10 000 annually in tax. This outcome is important for the stages that come next, because the $10 000 you save annually in tax is an extra $10 000 you can invest to push you into the further stages.

By this point you should already have a system around tracking your tax and deductions and be maximising deductions each year, but if you're starting to get serious around your money at the Focus stage, minimising tax should be your first priority.

Continuing with a level of regular super contributions will save you tax today and build your investments for the future. But again, until you purchase your first investment property, this strategy will likely take a back seat. Once you have your first property locked and loaded, you should revisit how much you're putting into your super with a view to bumping up your contributions.

Negative gearing is a strategy that comes into play at the Focus stage as you buy your first investment property. If you get it right, this strategy alone has the potential to hit your $10 000 annual tax-saving target. This strategy isn't limited to the tax benefits. Getting onto the property ladder and using leverage to accelerate your investing is the first huge step in becoming a Virgin Millionaire.

Before you jump into your first property investment you should be looking to leverage quality tax and investment advice so you make the most money from your investment and manage your risk well. You'll need to consider not just whether you do it or when but how much you spend, how you structure your borrowing and the type of property you choose. Once you buy a property these decisions can be difficult and expensive to unwind, so given the importance of this milestone on your Virgin Millionaire journey it's worth investing time and a few dollars in professional advice.

As mentioned above, property should be a key focus, but after your first investment property purchase you should be looking to crank up your regular investment plan. This means franked-dividend share investing will start to have more of an impact.

Tax strategies: Optimise

At the Optimise stage you'll continue to target a minimum of $10000 in annual tax saving, with the added goal of introducing at least one tax structure outside your superannuation fund. I'll unpack these structures in detail in the following chapter, but I'm referring to investment bonds, trusts and companies.

Using tax structures when you invest will limit the tax you'll pay on investment income this year and every year forever, so if you want to become a Virgin Millionaire, they'll be important for your continuing investment strategy. Be aware that tax structures can be incredibly effective but they can also be complicated and it's easy to make mistakes. I strongly suggest you combine introducing this strategy with getting advice so you get it right from the start.

At the Optimise stage your target is to invest 10 per cent of your household income in share-type investments. This is a significant amount of money so your wealth-building momentum will accelerate nicely. You'll consider franked-dividend share investing in the mix since reinvesting the tax saved will build your wealth faster. As I discuss in chapter 8, tax structures will add further upside.

Although it's not fully recommended for Virgin Millionaire purists, if you do own your own home at the Optimise stage, you should be seriously looking at debt recycling, particularly given you're going to be investing a significant amount of money in shares. Debt recycling is a serious accelerator, and for homeowners who are investing anyway this strategy is pretty much a no-brainer to save tax and get ahead faster.

Given your goal at the Optimise stage is to introduce multiple investment properties, the negative gearing tax benefits I've discussed in this chapter should be part of your planning. It will make a big difference to your rate of progress in the years ahead.

Tax strategies: Accelerate

At the Accelerate stage, your goal is to ensure you're not paying a dollar more than your fair share in tax, and to achieve this you're likely to decide to harness most of the strategies outlined in this chapter.

Franked-dividend share investing, negative gearing and debt recycling if you own your own home are all tactics that will drive significant tax savings. Because of the number of elements you have going on with your money at this stage and the complexity of their interplay, you'll benefit from working with an adviser or team of advisers. The right people will make you much more money than they charge.

Tax-saving investment structures should be a big focus at this stage as you seriously accelerate your wealth building and the balances in your investment holdings, and while you don't need your investment income to cover living expenses. Once you're using multiple tax structures, the benefits of having the right investments for the right structures are huge (as further discussed in the next chapter).

Tax strategies: Impact

Again, you should be using all the tools available to you to maximise your after-tax returns and legally minimise how much tax you pay.

At this point you'll want to have a crack dream team directing traffic with your tax planning and they should be prompting you should you need to change strategies. That said, it remains important that you maintain a firm grasp of your tax position and strategy.

Remember never to invest for tax purposes alone. I've lost count of the weird and complex tax-saving strategies out there and I've seen a number of people get so caught up with saving tax that they lose sight of what they're actually doing with their money. If you're looking at an investment that can help save you tax, the most important thing is that it's a good investment to begin with. Otherwise you'll get burned.

THE WRAP

Tax is one of the most important accelerators of your money, and it's an area you have to get right if you want to be a Virgin Millionaire. Not only is it important to make sure you're not paying more than your fair share, but being smart with your tax will give you more money you can invest to get ahead faster.

The tax rules can be complicated and confusing, but I hope that after reading this chapter you understand at least enough to take some smart next steps. Know that you can't (and shouldn't) try to do this on your own. As I've suggested, a good professional will be a profit driver, not an expense.

Tax is a knowledge area and skill set you will build over time, and it's one you need to take ownership of no matter how good the professionals in your corner might be. Every Virgin Millionaire needs to invest time and attention to understanding the tax rules and how to use them. The good news is that this investment will pay dividends tenfold, if not more.

Take action

Re-read the first section of this chapter until you're clear on the Australian marginal tax system, how it impacts your investing and the amount of after-tax income you have available to save.

Review your current approach to keeping records of your tax deductions and ensure they meet the criteria outlined in this chapter.

Set a calendar reminder for September and March to review your tax position and look at which tax strategies you can leverage in the current financial year.

Understand the key tax-saving strategies you can leverage, including negative gearing, debt recycling, franking credits and superannuation contributions.

Consider getting some quality advice around your tax and investment planning.

CHAPTER 8

Tax structures

The previous chapter should have given you a solid understanding of tax strategies and some tactics you can use to legally cut your tax bill. But I've saved the best for last. There's another lever that can save you significantly more tax dollars than any of the strategies we've covered so far.

On your journey to becoming a Virgin Millionaire, you're going to build an investment income that's likely to be well into six-figure territory. How much tax you pay on the income from that investment will have a big impact on how quickly it builds. And once built, how much tax you pay on the income will be a big driver of how much money you have to spend on your lifestyle.

Marginal tax rates

As you become a Virgin Millionaire you'll be building your investment income while still employed. For tax purposes your investment income is added to your employment income, which means it is taxed at your highest marginal rate, and may even push you into the next tax bracket. (Review Australian marginal tax rates shown in table 7.1.)

But it doesn't have to be this way.

When most people invest, they simply open an investment account and begin. This seems logical and if you didn't know better you could be forgiven for thinking this was the perfect way to get started.

When you open an investment account in your own name, you personally own all the investments and all the associated income. This means that as your investments start generating income through dividends or capital gains, the income is linked to your tax file number, you report it on your tax return and you pay tax at the appropriate marginal rate.

But *you* don't have to own your investments. When you open an investment account, you *could* own the account yourself, or you can choose to have that account owned by your partner or in joint names, or it can be owned by another tax entity altogether, such as under an investment bond, a company a trust or even your super fund.

Where you own your investments is important

To explain this concept I'm going to use a little bit of jargon (sorry). A tax entity is anything that has a tax file number (TFN) and lodges an annual tax return.

For example, every individual taxpayer in Australia has a TFN and completes (or should complete) a tax return each year. This means every individual is its own tax entity. Every super fund, company and trust also has a TFN and again is its own tax entity.

Different tax entities pay different rates of tax, and this creates an investment opportunity. Table 8.1 shows the tax rates available for a family and the different tax entities they could use to invest, as well as how much tax each would pay on $10 000 of investment income.

Table 8.1 tax rates across a family group

	Mum earning $145k	Dad earning $35k	15-year-old daughter earning $1.5k	18-year-old daughter earning $8k
Tax rate	Income – MTR* 39% capital gains – MTR with 50% discount available	Income – MTR 18% capital gains – MTR with 50% discount available	Income – MTR 47% capital gains – MTR w. 50% discount available	Income – MTR 0% capital gains – MTR w. 50% discount available
Tax payable on investment income of $10k	$3900	$1800	$4700	$0

	Super fund	Company	Trust	Investment bond
Tax rate	Income – 15% capital gains – 15% w. discount available to 10%	Income – 30% capital gains – 30% (no discount)	Variable based on where income is 'distributed'	Income max rate 30% capital gains @ 0% if held for 10 years+
Tax payable on investment income of $10k	$1500	$3000	n/a	$3000

* Marginal tax rate.

You can see from looking at the tax entities available to this family the difference between paying tax at the highest and the lowest rates is $4700 p.a. This means if you were to invest in the entity with the lowest tax rate rather than the highest, you would end up with an extra $4700 in after-tax investment returns every single year.

This extra money could be used to grow your investments faster or spend on your lifestyle today or a combination of both. Being smart with where you hold and own your investments makes a serious difference.

Most people invest without thinking too much about where they own investments. When you're just getting started this won't have much impact, but as your investments and your investment income grow, how much tax you pay will have an increasing impact on your progress.

Tax entities and structures

When most people think about saving on tax, they typically think about getting more tax deductions or finding out the latest tax hack to get a little bit more back in their tax return. But the reality is that there is a limit to how many tax deductions are available and there's a big opportunity to save a lot more tax.

If you want to be a successful investor your aim is, over time, to replace your employment salary with investment income. This means your goal is to build tens or even hundreds of thousands of dollars of annual investment income. When you're talking about this amount of money, doing even just a little bit better with your tax means a big dollar difference to your bottom line.

Think early about where you will own your investments and your tax structuring, since any change of ownership of your investments is considered a sale for tax purposes and therefore attracts capital gains tax. If you wait until you've already built a significant investment portfolio, it will become expensive to restructure the ownership to optimise your tax position. You need to be smart from the start to benefit down the line.

Using different tax entities and investment structures is *the* most powerful and effective way to save tax into the future. It's not the immediate sugar hit you get from finding a new tax deduction, but the amount of money you can make, or save, from getting this right into the years ahead is at least well into the hundreds of thousands of dollars.

I'll now outline the most common (and most useful) tax entities, how they work and how and when you can use them to your advantage. Once I've covered the key tax entities you need to be across, I'll talk you through these tax entities as you progress through the Smart Money Stages.

Super funds

Before we get into this, I want to call out that I completely get that superannuation may not seem a very exciting place to invest. If you're young and it will be decades before you can access your super, cranking up your super investments probably isn't high on your list of priorities.

But here's the thing. Super funds have the lowest tax rates of any investment entity. This means they're the most tax-effective place to invest.

A warning! I am going to get a bit deep on super but by the end of this section you'll understand why. First, I'm not suggesting you rush out and invest all your savings in super, because you're going to need other investments to hit some important Virgin Millionaire milestones.

The government wants you to save lots of money through your super fund. This isn't because they like you or because they're good people or because they particularly like super. They know that the wealthier you are when you retire, the less you'll rely on government benefits, and the more money you'll spend. And this means you'll generate more tax revenue to help fill their coffers.

To incentivise saving through super, the government offers reduced rates of tax for superannuation savings and investments. There are two main tax benefits. First, you receive tax deductions for putting money into your super and second, investment income generated inside your super fund is taxed at a lower rate.

Tax deductions on the way into superannuation

As discussed in detail in the tax strategies section, you can contribute money to your super fund every year and get significant tax deductions. Because these deductions mean it doesn't cost you $10k to get $10k into your super fund, your investment is larger than it would have been had you invested money outside your fund.

Lower tax rates inside your super fund

When thinking about superannuation, most people focus on the tax deductions, but the reality is that, over time, the lower tax rates *inside* your super fund will most likely make you even more money.

The tax rates that apply to super funds compared to personal rates are outlined in table 8.2.

Table 8.2 tax rates applicable on investment income

Type of investment income	Tax in accumulation phase (< age 60)	Tax in pension phase (age 60+)	Personal tax
Interest and dividend income	15%	0%	Marginal rates up to 47%
Capital gains	15%	0%	Marginal rates up to 47%
Capital gains on investments held for >12 months	10%	0%	Marginal rates up to 47% with 50% discount

The maximum rate of tax that applies to money invested in your super fund will be 15 per cent, with an even lower tax rate on capital gains made on your longer-term investments. It gets even better, because the tax rate drops to 0 per cent when you start a pension on your super money (discussed further below).

The 15 per cent tax rate is lower than personal marginal tax rates for anyone earning more than $18 200. And if you're a higher-income earner paying the top marginal tax rate of 47 per cent, the tax saving when you invest through super is a whopping 32 per cent. The lower rate of tax will have a significant impact on how quickly your investments grow.

Table 8.3 shows how your money would grow if you were to invest $10 000 annually from when you're 30 until you're 65. I've compared investing through your super fund against investing in your personal name and broken it down by income bracket. I've used the 30-year share market return of 9.8 per cent as the headline investment return, then applied the different tax rates to this income to calculate the after-tax investment return.

Table 8.3 investing $10 000 p.a. through super by tax bracket

	Super-annuation	Income $18.2k–$45k	Income $45k–$135k	Income $135k–$190k	Income $190k+
Tax rate	15%	18%	32%	39%	47%
After-tax investment return	8.33%	8.04%	6.66%	5.98%	5.19%
Investing $10k p.a.	$1 854 924	$1 738 854	$1 283 955	$1 109 614	$939 562

You can see that the difference in after-tax investment return is significant, from 5.19 per cent for the top marginal tax rate to 8.04 per cent if you're in the bottom marginal tax bracket. But note that all tax rates that apply on non-super investments are higher than superannuation, with the highest after-tax investment return of 8.33 per cent.

This flows through to overall investment growth, a massive $915 362 more when you invest through super for someone paying tax at the top personal marginal rate.

For the numbers people, it's worth noting that this example highlights the difference between super and personal investing and isn't intended to be a comprehensive breakdown. It's unrealistic to think that with over $1.5 million in investments you'd remain in the lowest tax bracket, because these investments would be generating income that would push you into the next tax bracket and beyond. The impact of this is that it understates superannuation benefits, meaning the real gap would be even greater.

It gets even better once you reach pension age

Under the superannuation rules, once you reach 60 you can start a 'pension' account with your super money. Once this pension is started the tax rate inside your super fund drops to zero on the first $1.9 million invested.

Based on $1.9 million in an investment account, you'd expect to be able to generate an annual income of around $95 000 (based on the 5 per cent rule). This translates to a tax-free income stream of $95 000 every single year.

If you were to earn an income of $95 000 in your personal name, under the current tax rules you'd pay $21 188.

By investing the money in your super fund instead of in your personal name, with the same investments and income you'd be better off by over $21 000 annually.

It's worth noting that this example assumes this $95 000 is your only personal income. If you have employment income, the tax you'd pay on this $95 000 if received in your personal name would be even higher. For example, if you have other income outside of superannuation of $95 000 annually, the tax that would apply on another $95 000 of investment income is $30 400 annually.

The government has made it harder and harder to put lots of money into super when you're old, so you don't want to wait until you're almost retired to focus on building up your superannuation. Drip the money in over years and decades and it will not only grow more but you'll ensure you take maximum advantage of the benefits available through superannuation.

As I've noted, I get that super is a little bit boring. I also get that most people think they probably don't need to worry too much about super until you're old. And this is partly true. But while your super is something that will become more important as you get older, and as you make more progress through the Smart Money Stages, the tax benefits of superannuation are compelling. While super probably shouldn't be the first place you invest, it also shouldn't be the last.

Superannuation wrap

Advantages:

- Maximum tax rate 15 per cent, lowest tax structure available
- Tax deductions for putting money into super
- All administration managed by your provider
- No costs to set up, low ongoing costs.

Disadvantages

- Investments are inaccessible until retirement age.

Average costs

- Establishment: free
- Ongoing: covered by super fund fees 0.2 per cent to 3 per cent of investment balance p.a. (average 0.9 per cent).

Investment bonds

An investment bond is an investment account you can use to buy shares, ETFs and funds. It is subject to some special rules and tax rates. These accounts work rather like superannuation funds but without the same restrictions on access.

Many people find it a little confusing that investment bonds, unlike the bonds that are covered in the sexy investments chapter, are a specific type of investment account. The naming conventions might throw you off.

They work similarly to a super fund in that within your investment bond account you can choose to invest in shares, ETFs and different managed investment funds.

The big benefit of investment bonds is their tax efficiencies. With an investment bond, you can invest capital gains tax-free when you invest for the long term. Further, all investment income (dividends) is taxed at a flat, lower tax rate, and this investment income isn't added to your personal tax return and therefore isn't taxed at marginal tax rates.

This significantly reduces the tax that applies to investment income received under an investment bond, and therefore increases your after-tax investment return. The higher your after-tax return, the faster you'll get ahead, the more progress you'll make in less time.

Historically, investment bonds have not been great. In the past they were expensive, they didn't offer great investment options and the admin and paperwork were really clunky.

But times have changed.

In recent years, with caps placed on superannuation balances and the ATO cracking down on trust investors, and with the development of more and better investment technologies, investment bonds have been reborn.

Today they have sharp pricing, quality investment options offering a range of quality funds and ETFs, and they have a decent user experience to boot.

Key rules of investment bonds

There are two main tax-related rules and benefits when it comes to investment bonds. First, when you hold the investment for 10 years or longer, capital gains tax doesn't apply. As a result, growth over the long term is entirely tax free, rather than being subject to marginal tax rates of up to 47 per cent.

Second, income such as dividends and interest from investment bonds isn't included in your tax return and instead is taxed internally by the fund. The maximum tax rate that applies is 30 per cent, which is lower than marginal tax rates on an income above $45 000. And if your aim is to build an investment income of tens of thousands of dollars into the future, this lower rate on your investment income will deliver serious tax savings.

Advantages of investment bonds

Investment bonds aren't right for everyone but if they are a fit for you they can really deliver.

I'll now unpack the numbers, comparing investing through one of these bonds against investing in your personal name.

Based on the long-term Australian share market return of 9.8 per cent, broken down as 4.8 per cent income and 5 per cent growth, the after-tax return looks like this:

Before-tax investment income (excluding growth) of 4.8 per cent, taxed at 30 per cent

After-tax income return = before-tax income × (1 − tax rate)

After-tax income return = 3.36 per cent [4.8 per cent × (1 − 30 per cent)]

Before-tax growth return = after-tax growth return: 5 per cent

Total after-tax return = 8.36 per cent (total tax 1.44 per cent)

Total tax rate: 14.7 per cent (1.44 per cent ÷ 9.8 per cent)

Personal investments

Compare this to investments owned in your personal name, assuming a personal tax rate of 32 per cent (the tax rate that applies when your income is above $45 000 p.a.):

Before-tax income of 4.8 per cent, taxed at 32 per cent

After-tax income return = before-tax income × (1 – tax rate)

After-tax income return = 3.264 per cent [4.8 per cent × (1 – 32 per cent)]

Before-tax growth 5 per cent, taxed @ marginal rate 32 per cent with 50 per cent long-term investing CGT discount

After-tax growth return = before-tax growth × (1 – tax rate) ÷ 2

After-tax growth return = 4.2 per cent [5 per cent × ((1 – 32 per cent) ÷ 2)]

Total after-tax return = 7.46 per cent (total tax 2.34 per cent)

Total tax rate: 23.9 per cent (2.34 per cent ÷ 9.8 per cent)

Based on these figures, you can see that the tax rate on investing through investment bonds is a whopping 9 per cent lower than investing in your personal name. That 9 per cent goes straight to your bottom line, helping your investments grow faster.

These figures are based on a taxable income of only $45 000 p.a. If your income (and therefore your tax rate) is higher, the benefits of bonds will be even greater. If you're building significant investments into the future, owning these investments in your personal name means you'll eventually be pushed into higher tax brackets and pay higher marginal tax rates. This means the benefits of investment bonds are likely to be significant.

Pro tip: If you're looking to invest money for your children, typically you'll add to these investments and have them grow until your children come of age. This long-term time frame lends itself fairly well to using investment bonds.

Investment bonds wrap

Advantages:

- Investment-income tax is capped at a maximum rate of 30 per cent.
- No capital gains tax applies when bonds are held for 10 years or longer.
- Investments can be accessed at any time.
- All administration is managed by your provider.
- There are no set-up costs and ongoing costs are low.

Disadvantages

- Investments need to be invested for 10 years+ before CGT discount applies.

Average costs

- Establishment: free
- Ongoing: 0.5 per cent – 3 per cent of investment balance p.a. (average 1 per cent) paid internally by investment bond.

Pty Ltd company

The most common form of company in Australia is an operating business that sells products or services. But companies can also be used for investment purposes, and because companies have a different tax rate from individuals this offers a tax-saving opportunity.

Pretty much anyone can start a company, so long as you're not on some government blacklist. You can do this pretty easily online or with the help of an accountant, and once the company is set up you can apply for a TFN. You can then open bank accounts or investment accounts and even buy property.

Investing through a company means that instead of the bank account or investment being held in your personal name, it's held in the name of the company and linked to its TFN.

Each year the company will file a tax return reporting investment income that will be taxed according to company-tax rules.

Pty Ltd companies pay a flat tax rate

Companies are subject to a flat rate of tax of 30 per cent—slightly lower than personal-tax rates plus Medicare levy if your personal income is above $45 000, but significantly lower than the personal-tax rate that applies in the higher tax brackets.

Table 8.4 shows different levels of income generated by investments in a company compared to income earned in your personal name, broken down by tax bracket.

You can see from these figures that if your tax rate and income are not particularly high, the benefits of using a Pty Ltd to invest are not high either and in some cases you'll actually be worse off. But as your investment income and tax rate increase, the benefits ramp up, pushing well into the tens of thousands of dollars each year.

Table 8.4 personal vs company income tax

	Pty Ltd	Income $18.2k–$45k	Income $45k–$135k	Income $135k–$190k	Income $190k+
Tax rate	30%	18%	32%	39%	47%
Tax payable on $50k p.a. income	$15 000	$9000	$16 000	$19 500	$23 500
Tax payable on $100k p.a. income	$30 000	$36 000	$32 000	$39 000	$47 000
Tax payable on $200k p.a. income	$60 000	$72 000	$74 000	$78 000	$94 000

This explains why this structure is favoured by those who have built or are looking to build significant wealth and investments.

Downsides of using a Pty Ltd to invest

A fairly significant downside to investing through a Pty Ltd company relates to capital gains tax. A company doesn't qualify for the 50 per cent capital gains tax discount for investments held for longer than 12 months, which means that when you sell your investments in a company you will pay more tax than you would were those investments in your personal name.

If you're investing through a company into an index fund or ETF you're planning to hold forever, the impact may be minimal but it's worth being aware of.

One more thing to consider is that land tax on property is higher if the investment is in the name of a company rather than an individual. Because the mechanics of this are complicated, I suggest you get good tax advice before proceeding but the short version is that because of the higher tax rate as well as the inability to access the capital-gains tax discount, investing in property through a company is unlikely to be the best move for a Virgin Millionaire.

Pty Ltd company wrap

Advantages:

- Flat rate of tax on income is capped at 30 per cent.
- Ability to borrow money

Disadvantages:

- It costs to set up and file a tax return each year.
- Administration time is needed to manage the investment.
- The 50 per cent capital-gains discount for investments held for 12 months or more does not apply.
- If the investment involves buying property, there's no land tax exemption.

(continued)

Costs:

- Establishment: $500 – $1000 one off (average $750)
- Ongoing tax returns and management: $1000 – $3000 (average $1500 p.a.)

Discretionary trusts

Because trusts are a tax entity that allows flexibility around tax planning, they're the most common tax structure used by people with significant wealth.

You establish your trust, register it and get a tax file number, and once this is done you can invest money in the name of the trust. Once you have a TFN you can open bank accounts and share investing accounts, buy property, take out mortgages or set up any other investments that take your fancy.

Once you own investments under, or inside, your trust, they will generate income and when they're eventually sold they will generate capital gains. This income is taxable. The main rule of a trust is that the income needs to be distributed to another beneficiary.

A beneficiary can be any individual but the most common are family members. You can also distribute income to a Pty Ltd company (as already discussed) and this can save a serious amount of tax.

How trusts work

Investing through a trust typically works like this. You build investments by making an initial contribution of money to the trust, or regular deposits, or both. The money is then invested and generates an investment income that is distributed each year.

Say, for example, you set up a $2 million investment portfolio in a trust that delivers an annual investment income of $100 000 (table 8.5). You need to decide to which beneficiaries that income will be distributed to (see table 8.1 for examples of potential beneficiaries).

Tables 8.5 to 8.7 set out the potential benefits of a trust and investment company structure. In this example, the trust is generating $100 000 of annual investment income. The examples in tables 8.5 and 8.6 show a benefit from using a trust, and in the example in table 8.7 there is no benefit from using this structure.

In the table 8.5 scenario, using a trust allows this family to split their distributions between an older child and one parent, generating a tax saving within that year of $5637. It's highly likely there will be benefits from using a trust in future years as the second child gets older and is able to receive investment income distributions without paying tax at the top marginal tax rate.

Table 8.5 example 1—family with older children

	Mum earning $145k	Dad earning $25k	13-year-old daughter with no income	18-year-old daughter earning $8k	Company	Total
Tax rate	39%	18%	47%	0%	30%	
Investment income distribution paid		$63 000		$37 000		$100 000
Tax on distribution		$19 900		$4863		$24 763
Where income would be received without a trust		$100 000				$100 000
Tax on income without a trust		$30 400				$30 400
Trust benefit						**$5637 p.a.**

In the scenario in table 8.6 (overleaf), not only are both parents (investors) in the top marginal tax bracket but their children, too, would be required to pay tax at the top marginal rate because they are still minors. However, investment income can be distributed to an investment company, delivering an annual tax benefit of $17 000.

Table 8.6 example 2—high-income couple with young kids

	Mum earning $190k	Dad earning $210k	2-year-old daughter	6-year-old daughter	Company	Total
Tax rate	47%	47%	47%	47%	30%	
Investment income distribution paid					$100 000	$100 000
Tax on distribution					$30 000	$30 000
Where income would be received without a trust		$100 000				$100 000
Tax on income without a trust		$47 000				$47 000
Trust benefit						**$17 000 p.a.**

In the third example (table 8.7), there are no children to whom funds might be distributed and one investor is already at the 39 per cent tax rate, so no benefit would be taken from distributing funds to them. If a trust were in place, distributing funds between Dad and an investment company would result in the greatest possible reduction in tax paid. If there was no trust in place, the investment income could be owned solely by the lower income earner and the tax paid would be $1925 more than that paid under the trust scenario.

Table 8.7 example 3—couple with lower income earner and no kids

	Mum earning $145k	Dad earning $25k	Company	Total
Tax rate	39%	0%	30%	
Investment income distribution paid		$20 000	$80 000	
Tax on distribution		$4475	$24 000	$28 475
Where income would be received without a trust		$100 000		
Tax on income without a trust		$30 400		$30 400
Trust benefit				**$1925**

As I will discuss, when you use any tax entity you need to consider the costs of establishing and operating it. In this case, because it's unlikely the tax benefit of $1925 would cover the trust costs, the trust is likely to be an unnecessary and ineffective addition to the investment strategy.

Recapping trusts

Trusts can be an effective way to distribute investment income and reduce the tax paid on this income. Trusts are particularly beneficial if your income fluctuates from year to year or if you have children who will at some point be able to receive trust income distributions.

If your income levels and tax rates change from year to year, a trust will enable you to change your distribution strategy to deliver the best after-tax outcomes. And if you're a high-income couple and think you may have adult children to distribute trust income to in the future, you can lean on your investment company while you build wealth and change your strategy when it's beneficial to do so.

The beauty of a discretionary trust is that you can change the beneficiaries each year based on what will deliver the best after-tax outcome. This allows you to optimise the after-tax return across your family and investment entities each year into the future. This flexibility is why this tax structure is the most popular one for wealthy investors.

Trusts wrap

Advantages:

- Investment income can be split across multiple taxpayers.
- Beneficiaries can be changed each year to optimise tax outcomes.
- It is possible to borrow inside a trust.

Disadvantages:

- There are costs involved with setup and with annual tax returns.
- Administration can be time-consuming.
- There is no land-tax exemption when investing in property.

(*continued*)

Costs

- There is a one-off establishment cost of $1k to $5k or more (average $3k), depending on complexity.
- Ongoing tax returns and management cost $2k to $5k or more (average $3k p.a.)

Private ancillary funds

A private ancillary fund or PAF is a private investment trust usually set up for the purposes of charitable giving. This is generally something you'd only consider once you're either in or getting close to the Impact stage because you've decided you want to gift some of your money.

The big benefit of a PAF is that any money you contribute can be claimed as a full tax deduction in the year the contribution is made. Let's say you have a significant capital gain from selling an investment or you've sold a business. You'd be able to access an immediate tax deduction at the same time as kick-starting charitable giving.

If giving is something that's part of your ideal future lifestyle, my strong suggestion is that as you start getting into the more advanced Smart Money Stages you seek out some quality advice about PAFs and whether this structure could be beneficial for you.

Private ancillary fund wrap

Advantages:

- A contribution is eligible for a full tax deduction.
- You can give to charitable causes that are important to you.
- You have full control of your investments.

Disadvantages:

- Money is given away once it enters this structure.
- Some administration time will be required.

Costs

- There is a one-off establishment cost of $2k to $10k or more, depending on complexity (average $5k).
- Ongoing tax returns and management will cost from $4k to $10k or more (average $6k).

How to figure out if entities are worth it?

If you're thinking about setting up a trust, company or multiple tax entities, you need to be sure the benefits outweigh the costs.

Not only are there costs involved with setup but there are ongoing management costs, including annual tax returns. These costs may run into thousands of dollars and, over the life of the entity, into the tens of thousands. If you're receiving chunky tax benefits from optimising your investments, these costs can easily be offset, but if your investing is in its early stages the costs can outweigh the benefits.

The exception is investment bonds, which are typically free to set up and have low ongoing costs. Because the cost hurdle is lower, you may find this to be a good place to begin with tax entities.

If you are considering using any tax entity, do your research and ensure you understand fully the costs and downsides as well as the benefits. Get advice, but not necessarily from an accountant who stands to be paid a fee if you go ahead. You need to be sure your adviser is objective.

Smart Money Stages and tax structures

Once again, the right approach when it comes to tax entities and tax structures will be dictated by what's going on with your money and the Smart Money Stage you've reached. Table 8.8 outlines the key considerations at each stage.

Table 8.8 Smart Money Stages and tax structures

Success outcomes	Foundations	Focus	Optimise	Accelerate	Impact
Tax	Leverage at least one strategy to save a minimum $1k p.a. in tax.	Leverage multiple tax strategies to save a minimum $10k p.a. in tax.	Investment strategy to include at least one tax structure outside of superannuation (e.g. bonds, trust, company etc.).	Be 100% confident you're not paying more than your fair share of tax.	You have multiple tax-saving structures in place, including PAF.

Foundations: Tax structures

At the Foundations stage you probably don't need to worry too much about tax structures as, for two reasons, most of them won't yet be beneficial. First, because you won't have that much money invested you won't have that much investment income. Second, you will need access to the money you do have to buy your first property.

That said, getting the tax structuring of your investments right from the start will make you serious money into the future, so whether or not you decide to use tax entities, you should be clear on the tax-structuring options available.

If you're starting from a strong position with surplus savings in the thousands of dollars each month, you can scratch what I've just said and accelerate your consideration of tax entities asap.

You may consider an investment bond at this stage, particularly if you're saving or investing for children. The low costs to set up and manage this tax structure mean there isn't a big downside, but given the benefits only really kick in when the money is invested for 10 years or more, only use this tax structure with money not needed for shorter-term investing goals.

One thing you should seriously consider at this stage is starting to use your lowest tax-paying investment account in your super fund, even if it's with a minimal level of contributions of $5 or $10 a month. This will get you more focused on your super fund and start building the muscle that will deliver big benefits in the future.

Tax structures: Focus

At the Focus stage, your big goal is the purchase of your first investment property. Any property purchase is a large investment so it's critical the tax structuring is right. Given the impact this investment will have on your financial position and your Virgin Millionaire progress, consider getting good advice to deliver the ideal outcome.

Given where you are in your investing journey at this stage, it's unlikely you'll be using a trust or investment company for this purchase. However, if you are in a relationship, whether the property is owned in one name or jointly will make a big difference to future after-tax returns. This key decision should be considered carefully.

Once your property has been purchased, it will be time to focus again on building share-type investments. Because you'll be looking both to grow these investments and at how much you'll be investing in the years ahead, it's important you get the tax structuring right. You may want to consider using an investment bond or trust at this point. Before doing this it's important that you understand the benefits and costs compared to investing in your personal name, and how this fits in with your plan over the short, medium and longer term.

After your property purchase you should also reconsider your super contributions strategy and whether it's appropriate to increase your use of this tax-saving structure.

Tax structures: Optimise

At the Optimise stage, the right tax structuring becomes even more valuable for a couple of reasons. First, because you have more investments and wealth behind you, the benefits are more significant.

Second, because you're aiming to buy further property at the same time as you're increasing your share investing to 10 per cent of your household income, your future investments have larger numbers attached to them. From here in it will become increasingly expensive to restructure your investments so you'll want to set everything up correctly before you crack on.

Investment bonds are likely to be part of your strategy at this stage for investments you're planning to hold for the long term. This will give you the benefit of both a reduced tax rate on investment income in the short term and no capital gains tax once you've held the investments for 10 years or more.

Depending on your income level, savings capacity and existing investments, you should also consider a trust plus investment company combo—but before you do this, get a good adviser *and* a good accountant in your corner.

At this stage you will also be looking to ramp up your super contributions to the maximum limit each year to take advantage of the lowest tax environment for investing and to maximise your annual tax deductions.

Tax structures: Accelerate

At the Accelerate stage you should be leveraging the elements already in play from the Optimise stage, which by now will be delivering solid tax savings. But the most important focus is setting your sights on the Impact stage and the smart money freedom around the corner. Start positioning your investments and tax structuring in ways that will deliver the ideal outcomes at the next stage and as far as possible into the future to avoid the need to restructure when you reach the next Smart Money Stage.

Investment bonds, trusts and investment companies will all deliver increasing benefits, but remember there's no one 'right' way to set things up that works best for everyone. The right way for you will depend on exactly where you're at, the lifestyle you want to live now and into the future, and what's important to you.

The interplay between different tax structures, your goals and your lifestyle is complex and has many elements that are hard for even the most experienced Virgin Millionaire to manage alone. If you haven't already done so, you should now consider engaging high-quality professional help to get the most out of the money you have and set things up in the ideal way for you.

Tax structures: Impact

To have reached the Impact stage you will have already taken the time to understand how, where and when different tax structures will help you get more out of the money you have. This knowledge will be helpful as you move through the Impact stage into true smart money freedom, but keep in mind that the approach that got you to this point may not be the best approach for this stage and what's ahead.

While your investments and wealth are likely to continue to grow through this stage, things may become simpler if and when you decide to wind back on work (and your employment income). You may be able to reduce and simplify the tax structures and entities you have in place to make things easier, and cheaper, to manage.

Whether or not this happens for you, it's going to be important to stay on top of your tax planning and structuring so you continue to pay no more than your fair share in tax. With the level of wealth you have behind you now, the optimal structuring will have a big impact on your bottom line.

Take the time at the Impact stage to understand how a PAF could work for you. Depending on your giving goals, this entity could help you achieve them and save tax. It should go without saying that you should introduce any other new entity only after careful consideration and quality advice.

THE WRAP

Most people don't understand tax well enough to make it work for them. But once you understand the rules and how to use them to your advantage you can seriously accelerate your progress and get more from the money you already have.

Some people I talk to about their money complain about the tax rules in Australia, considering some of them to be unfair. The reality is you can either choose to use the rules that exist to your advantage, or you can choose to be left behind or be forced to work harder to achieve the same result. Both these latter choices are far from ideal, or at the very least not the kind of smart that's needed to become a Virgin Millionaire.

I mentioned in chapter 7 that your knowledge around tax strategies is a skill set you build over time. The same applies to tax structures. It will take time to build this knowledge, but the good news is that your understanding will ramp up as you progress through the Smart Money Stages. This means you can build your knowledge while you build your investments until all your ducks are in a row.

I hope after reading this book you will have a better understanding of tax and the key rules and tactics you will need to be across. Since most of the learning around tax will come from putting these ideas into practice and starting to flex your tax muscle, it's going to be highly beneficial to get started as soon as possible.

Take action

- Decide where you will own your investments, as that will have a big impact on how much tax you pay, your after-tax investment returns and how much money you can reinvest to grow your investments faster.

- Understand the tax concessions that make superannuation the most tax-effective place to invest.

- Learn about investment bonds and how they can increase your after-tax investment return.

- Understand the tax rules for investing through a Pty Ltd company and how the flat tax rate can be helpful as your investment income grows.

- Learn how a trust can enable flexibility in your investing to manage and reduce investment tax.

- Understand the true costs of different tax entities so you can identify when they will deliver benefits in excess of costs.

- Consider engaging a professional to assist you with leveraging tax structures to grow your investments faster.

CHAPTER 9

Your Virgin Millionaire roadmap

I have a confession to make. I've always been a planner, but recently I let things slip.

I've been investing since I first got into financial planning. And for the past 10 years, since I started going deep into detailed short- and long-term planning with my clients, I've always had rock-solid short- and long-term savings, investing, debt and super targets.

But a couple of years ago there were a bunch of things going on financially and for me personally, and I stopped planning.

My wife Yang and I had just had our second child, following our first in quick (unplanned) succession. For anyone who's been in this position, no explanation is really needed. If you haven't you can take my word — it's chaos.

COVID was then raging, which was disrupting work significantly. Dealing with lockdowns, remote work, returning to non-remote work, close-contact isolation and all the rest of it was a challenge. At the same time, my business and our team had grown significantly through the COVID years, and I was trying to learn a new role as a leader and manager while still wearing all my other hats.

Fair to say, then, there were a lot of things competing for my attention. As a result, I let a few things slip, one of which was my money planning. And that's a slippery slope.

Good habits are hard to form but very easy to break, and through this period I let a lot of the hard work I'd put in over almost a decade unravel. First, Yang and I stopped doing our monthly Smart Money Review. That was easy to explain. What with chronic lack of sleep with the new baby, being stretched for time with work, and dealing with the COVID disruptions, it was easy for us to justify pushing this conversation out to a tomorrow that never seemed to come around.

Things continued to tick along okay. Our savings were still growing, albeit at a slower rate than they had in the past. We were still investing, but not as regularly or consistently as before. And we were still being smart with our tax, though we weren't as on top of our tax planning as we had been in previous years.

Again, all these little things were easy enough for us to justify.

The next thing that slipped was our quarterly check-ins, and shortly after the annual planning session was indefinitely postponed. Before we knew it, a year had gone by.

At that point we were feeling a bit lost. We knew there were a few things we weren't doing that we probably should have been. We weren't feeling as on top of things as we wanted to be. And we could tell that our progress had slowed, which was odd given our incomes had increased through this period.

But once the bad habits had set in, it took some serious work to get back on track.

Oddly, the real catalyst for us was writing my last book, *Replace Your Salary by Investing*. As I was writing I was reminded of the power of compounding, both around investing but more around habits. Particularly around the habits, I remembered when our personal money and planning seemed almost effortless.

Our results were flowing. We were hitting most of our milestones, and meeting or exceeding most of our targets. I wanted that back, so I had a chat with Yang and we blocked out time in our calendars to make this happen.

It wasn't easy. The planning part was fine, but when it came time to putting our ideas into practice we quickly started making excuses. We had to call out our slack behaviour and push on, and I can tell you it took some pushing.

But the results were worth it. In the two years since, we've rebuilt our previous habits and systems around our money so they're once again effortless. Our investments have grown more in the past two years than in the previous five, which has made our next property purchase possible much sooner than we'd planned.

To share a learning from this experience, I feel like the one thing we did that had the biggest impact was reintroducing a regular weekly investment plan. We'd had one going in the past, but with variable cashflow through COVID we decided it was best to pause this payment. That pause quickly turned into a break, then it just went off our radar altogether.

When we reintroduced weekly investing a couple of years ago, the amount we were investing was less than it had been previously. But the fact this was happening weekly immediately got us both more focused on our investing. It gave us something positive to talk about at our Smart Money Review and motivated us to do more.

We quickly increased our regular investment amount by cutting out a couple of random expenses we had collected that we weren't getting much value or enjoyment out of. We then wanted to do more but didn't want to cut more expenses, so we put a plan in place to increase our incomes, setting some targets around this that would make it possible.

We pushed hard to make that happen, after which we were able to further increase our investments. We are now investing over 400 per cent more than we did before COVID. Our financial trajectory has increased more in this period than it ever had in the past, and that in turn has opened up new possibilities for investing.

The thing with planning is that it's easier to *not* do it today than it is to carve out the time to put in the work and make it happen. It's easy to fall into the trap of thinking that if there's no immediate quantifiable upside, the time (or money) you spend on this won't be worth it.

But this couldn't be further from the truth.

A good financial plan can make you a bunch of money straight away. It can help you save tax, choose better investments, access better investment products and accounts, save interest costs, and leverage tax structures and strategies to make you money.

It's this immediate, quantifiable return on investment that most people think about when they consider setting up a financial plan. But in my experience, there are other benefits that will make you so much more money.

For Yang and me, the boost in money progress we were now enjoying was *not* from implementing some sexy tax-saving strategy, or anything wildly different from what we'd been doing in the past. The real benefit came from being more focused on our money and our saving and investing bottom line.

Planning helps you set goals and targets around your money, then gives you the benchmark for seeing how well you're tracking towards these targets. This is the core of your money 'system' and is the foundation everything else is built on.

As a prospective Virgin Millionaire, you have to *work* towards your version of smart money freedom. It will take years, probably decades. The only way you'll make it through those years and actually take the action that's needed to get the results you want is by maintaining a consistent focus on your money.

You need to concentrate on your saving and spending, making sure this stays inside the guardrails you've set. Keep your investments building and crank the power of compounding. Get set for property purchases at the earliest possible (appropriate) opportunity to use the power of leverage effectively. Use the tax rules to your advantage every single year to keep more of your hard-earned income and maximise the after-tax return on your investments. And manage your risk.

When you do all this, you will be using your money to its full potential and making maximum progress in the shortest time possible.

A dose of truth serum here: as much as it would be nice, it's crazy to imagine this outcome will 'just happen' without your actively driving it.

Before we move on to the next section, I should admit that as a professional financial planner I'm a bit (maybe more than a bit) biased. But as you can see from my own story, and as I hope you'll learn from what follows, the power and value of having a rock-solid plan at each point on your Virgin Millionaire journey is *huge*.

To be clear, when I refer to having a plan, I'm not necessarily talking about a financial plan developed with a financial planner; I mean, rather, that you're clear on where you're headed with your money, and you know what you need to do to get there.

Benefits of having a plan

Planning with your money is important, but any time you're investing time, money or both, it's important you benefit through a return on this investment. To help you get clear on when planning will be most valuable for you, I've broken down the benefits of having a plan and where and how they'll benefit you.

Make you money

Now I know I just said that you shouldn't fall into the trap of thinking the *only* reason you'd do a financial plan is to make an immediate return on investment (ROI). But the reality is that most of the time there *will* be an immediate ROI, and often this will run into thousands of dollars at least.

Quantifiable areas in which you make money from a financial plan include:

- **tax strategies.** Make money from implementing the right strategies at the right time, cutting your tax bill and keeping more of your income.
- **tax structures.** Increase your after-tax investment return by reducing the tax paid on your investment income.
- **save more.** You'll save more money by following a solid approach to your saving and spending plan (budget), then running a robust savings system.
- **invest more.** Backed up by a solid plan, you'll invest more money sooner and therefore benefit more from compounding.
- **better investment performance.** With the right investment approach you'll avoid reactive investment decisions and underperforming investments, ultimately making more money from your investments.
- **cheaper products.** By reviewing your super fund, investment account, mortgage, banking products and insurances, you'll ensure they are delivering good value for money and that you're not paying more than you have to.
- **no commission.** Using a no-commission adviser for insurance products makes the products cheaper for you.
- **reduce risk.** With a solid approach to your risk management, you'll avoid the cost of being forced to sell investments at the wrong time.

Further to these quantifiable areas, there are a number of things that will make you money from your financial plan but are a bit harder to measure.

Non-quantifiable areas in which you make money from a financial plan include:

- **game plan.** Knowing you're on top of everything and understanding where you're headed allows you to optimise your financial trajectory.
- **confidence.** Being 100 per cent confident in your strategy and direction means you'll take more action sooner.
- **framework.** A framework allows you to assess your options and make the very best choices for you.
- **balance.** Find balance between your money progress and your personal goals.
- **save time.** By having a solid plan you'll cover the bigger-picture thinking and save a heap of time when it comes to its execution, and this time saving is multiplied by using professional advisers.
- **accountability.** Your plan will keep you accountable for your results, meaning better outcomes in less time. This accountability will be amplified if you have a professional supporting the execution of your plan.
- **professional network.** A good plan will alert you when you need other money professionals, such as for tax, mortgages or wills), and will help set you up for success in your work with them.

Don't expect all these things to come up for you each month, or even each year, but with so many elements you only need one of them to be relevant for you to enjoy a serious financial upside.

And beyond the more variable and shorter-term factors, some elements will deliver consistent benefits every single year, which is why it's so important to go through the planning process regularly.

Your financial trajectory

One of the core principles of money success and becoming a Virgin Millionaire is that you need to know how much you want to spend on your ideal lifestyle, how much you need in investments to deliver you that income year on year, the current path you're on and where you're headed with your money — that is, your financial trajectory.

If you don't have a plan, you won't know where you need to get to, when you can expect to get there and whether you're on track.

This means one of the first things you need to do with your money is to get clear on your trajectory. I touched on this earlier but want to reinforce how important it is here.

There's a quote of uncertain origin that I think sums this up perfectly:

A dream without a goal is a wish. A goal without a plan is just a dream.

For most people, the first time you map out your financial trajectory you probably won't be on track to end up exactly *where* you want to *when* you want to (sorry). And when you fully map out your ideal lifestyle spending, you probably won't be on track for that either.

Knowing you're not on track is a good thing, because it will tell you how big the gap is between the path you're currently on and where you want to be. This gap will dictate exactly what action you need to take to close the gap.

To establish your financial trajectory, you'll need to make some assumptions about the future, such as your investment returns and saving rates, how your income will grow and other key variables.

At Pivot Wealth we start with the following assumptions:

- income growth rate (age 20–50): 3 per cent
- income growth rate (age 50+): no growth
- share investment return: 8 per cent
- property return: 5 per cent
- cash return: 1 per cent
- superannuation return (age 20–50): 8 per cent
- superannuation return (age 50+): 6.5 per cent.

When doing this, keep in mind that life and investment markets don't follow straight lines, and it doesn't matter how smart and considered your assumptions are, reality is going to be slightly different—and that's totally okay.

What's important here is that we use conservative assumptions that you're likely to exceed. This way you're not putting too much pressure on your plan. You should be totally confident it won't be investment markets or your money that mean you fall short of your targets, only your *actions*.

Assess the impact of making changes

There are a lot of different ways to be right when it comes to your money, but there's only one right way for you. You may be thinking about starting an investment portfolio or investing through your super fund or paying down debt or buying a property. Each of these actions will have a different financial outcome attached to it.

Understanding the financial upside of doing different things with your money is an important part of making good money choices, but how much money you can make isn't the only important consideration.

As noted in the discussion on leverage in chapter 2, when you crunch your numbers, debt is *the* strategy that will always 'win'. But debt is the *worst* strategy when it comes to lifestyle and risk. The more debt you have, the more of your income you need to allocate to covering debt repayments. Further, the more debt you have, the more risk you carry around interest rates, inflation and cashflow commitments. This means maximum debt is unlikely to be the best strategy for you.

On the flip side, not using debt at all means you're leaving a *lot* of money on the table, your money won't be working to its full potential and you'll make slower progress towards smart money freedom.

Somewhere between maximum debt and no debt you'll find the right level for you. Finding the right level of debt is one of the most important elements of a solid plan for your money, and the sooner you find this point the sooner you'll start maximising your rate of financial progress.

But your ideal debt level depends on *you*—what's going on with your money, what's important to you, and the lifestyle you want to live now and into the future.

The only way to figure out the ideal debt level for you is through a solid planning approach. I promise you that figuring out what this debt level is as quickly as possible, then positioning your money to get to that point at the earliest possible opportunity, will make you a lot of money.

This is one of the main reasons why planning is so important.

Tax is another area where it's almost impossible to make quality choices without a rock-solid financial plan. In the previous chapter I covered the huge opportunity that exists to save tax through using different tax structures, such as investment bonds, trusts and companies, and superannuation.

Each of these tax structures can save you tens or sometimes even hundreds of thousands of dollars in tax each year. But each different tax structure has different rules, benefits and downsides that dictate whether and when they will work well for you. The only way to accurately assess whether you should include these tax structures in your investing, or which tax structures will be the most beneficial, is by mapping their impact on the other things you're doing with your money.

When considering other money, investing and strategy options, to make the best choice you need to look at the upside along with the potential downsides and risks.

And then there's your lifestyle planning. Through the course of your life you'll need to make lots of big personal choices: which school to get your kids into, how much parental leave to take, buying or upgrading your home, and a bunch of other things in between. When making these decisions, your aim is to ensure they fit with your money and don't compromise your financial progress more than you're comfortable with.

To determine whether a big lifestyle or spending choice actually fits your means and needs and what's going on with your money, you have to assess its impact on your financial trajectory. This is the only way you can ensure these decisions don't derail your financial progress.

By the later Smart Money Stages you should have set up your investments to deliver enough money to cover your ideal lifestyle spending. At this point you're still building your investments, and every time you increase your spending it reduces your financial trajectory, which then needs to be balanced with more investing to increase your trajectory again.

This is a process of iteration in which you need to look at the investing upside alongside lifestyle and spending choices. The only way you can do this with any degree of accuracy and confidence is by understanding the numbers. Without a solid planning approach to guide your thinking as you work through these choices, you'd really just be *guessing*. Given the importance of these decisions, and the gravity of the impact on your money, guessing would be borderline reckless.

Your lifestyle choices are largely personal, but they do come with a significant financial impact that should be considered as part of your planning. Here again, the numbers won't be the only driver of your choices, but given how significant the impact of these decisions is, the numbers shouldn't be ignored.

A while back I was working with a couple who weren't on top of their planning before we met, and not being across their numbers ended up being seriously costly for them.

Pete and Paula were young executives, both with good jobs, earning good money. In their late twenties they set a goal of buying a home, and were planning on starting a family in a few years' time. They were saving strongly and had already purchased an investment property. They were also doing some regular investing, which was going well.

They built up their savings and investing until they had enough money to buy their home. To buy the home they wanted, a lovely terrace house in

Sydney's inner west, they sold their investment property and shares. They had stretched themselves a bit to buy a home they really loved, and they were stoked.

If Pete and Paula had put a plan in place at this point, either on their own or with the help of a financial planner, it wouldn't have made them any money. Because they were focused on selling investments and buying a home, there would have been no immediate return on investment (ROI).

This puts a lot of people off actually setting up a plan. I totally understand that if you're thinking about spending money to get some help with your finances, you want to be able to see a clear ROI. But in this case the real return for this couple on doing a plan was hidden well below the surface ...

After Pete and Paula's property purchase their focus shifted back to building up their savings. They wanted to create a buffer and put some things into place to allow them to start a family. They had their first daughter about two years later. Maternity leave was tight, covering their mortgage payments and living on a reduced income, but they were expecting this and made it work well enough.

But this is where the real problems started bubbling to the surface.

After the birth of their daughter Paula fell in love with being a mum. This shifted her priorities around her career, and she decided she wanted to return to work only in a part-time capacity until they had their second child, which they were planning to do in a couple of years' time.

When Paula returned to work, childcare costs started kicking in, and this along with Paula's part-time income was creating a real challenge. They were struggling to make ends meet day to day *and* keep up with their mortgage payments *and* cover childcare costs, not to mention putting away some extra savings to cover the next round of maternity leave.

Saving had slowed a while back and investing had stopped altogether, and the more time Pete and Paula spent looking at their numbers, the more concerned they became. They realised quickly they wouldn't be able to have another child, cope with another round of maternity leave and cover another set of childcare fees without making some significant changes.

Long story short, Pete and Paula decided they didn't want to compromise on their family planning, and they would need to sell their home to make this possible. They had built up some equity in their property over time, so when Pete and Paula sold the house they got a nice cash injection that gave them some breathing room.

There is a happy ending here. We started working together about a year later and soon got things back on track. When I started crunching the numbers, I realised how large a price Pete and Paula had paid for this string of decisions — it was well over a million dollars.

Because they sold down all their investments to make their home purchase work, they ended up in a position where they had a lovely home, but no investment assets behind them. This was the first area that cost them a bunch of money. But there were more...

They also had to pay selling costs on exiting their investment property, purchase costs to buy their home, then selling costs on the same property, and purchase costs on another, similar investment property in the future. These costs totalled over $100k. Given how early they were on their investing journey, this is money they could have had growing for them over the years to make a heap of extra money.

This $100k alone, if invested from age 30 to 65 and assuming the long-term share market return of 9.8 per cent and a tax rate of 30 per cent, would have grown to $1 095 902.

Beyond this, there was the cost of not having their investment property growing for them in the five years between the time they sold it and eventually purchased another property. What's more, the property market was increasing throughout this time, which meant that when they did eventually get back into the property market they ended up paying more for less.

Thankfully we got things back on track for Pete and Paula, but the reality was that the pathway they took cost them *a lot* of money. With the new plans they had around their family, that extra million bucks or so would have been pretty helpful.

Hindsight is a wonderful thing, and if we could make all our decisions this way I'm sure we'd all be a lot richer than we are right now. Pete and Paula could have done things slightly differently and it would have drastically changed their outcomes.

After going through the planning process with them, they confessed to me they were kicking themselves for their lack of planning at the time they made their home purchase decision.

There were two options they could have considered. The first was to spend less on their home, at a level that would have allowed them to preserve their investment property and have a lesser impact on their cashflow after the property purchase.

The second option would have been to delay their home purchase until their numbers stacked up.

Both of these options were absolutely less ideal for Pete and Paula from a lifestyle perspective. They wanted that lovely home, and they wanted to start a family. But if they'd realised the true cost there's no way they would have followed the path they did.

This is the power of a good plan.

Whenever you're making money decisions, big lifestyle choices or investments, you need to understand your numbers, along with the risks and downsides, to make the best choice for you.

Motivating you to take action

It's great to have a great plan, but even the world's best financial plan is worthless if you don't *take action*. Only then will the results start to build, so set up that savings account, bump up your savings or investment rate, ditch that debt or buy your next property... or whatever is the next step in your plan.

Action is crucial. What that action is, how much action you take and how quickly you take it are the main variables that will dictate your rate of financial progress moving forward.

The first step is to map your financial trajectory. The next is to assess the impact of the different pathways before you and your money. Once you've chosen the path you want to take in the short term, take it.

But without a solid plan for your money, it's almost impossible to know what pathway forward is going to be the best one for you. And without having total confidence in this path, you're going to doubt yourself and most likely be paralysed by the fear of choosing the wrong path and making a costly mistake. Lacking confidence, you don't take as much (or any) action, and then you don't get the results you're looking for.

It's only with a good plan for your money and investments that you're going to have enough confidence to take maximum action and get maximum results.

On the flip side, knowing where you want to get to, having explored the paths you can take to get there and chosen the path forward you're most comfortable with, you put yourself in a position of strength. From this position you should be ready to go out there 'guns blazing' and take prompt, confident action to start cranking your money.

This action is going to make you serious money over time, but it's not the quick 'sugar-fix' that most people think about when they consider putting a financial plan in place. Maybe there's no immediate ROI on the decisions you make, no sexy tax strategies or investment upside, but the benefits of the work you do here are likely to make you hundreds of thousands (if not millions) of dollars over the years ahead.

A benchmark for tracking progress

Once you get clear on your financial trajectory and start moving forward, you need to check in regularly on your results. This is the only way you'll be able to tell if your plan is working, and it's absolutely crucial to drive your motivation.

When this element of your planning is working as it should, once you have a solid plan in place for your money, you know exactly where your money should be 'at' looking forward. You should be clear on how much you'll have in savings, investments and debt, and on your overall wealth position looking forward.

Being clear on your trajectory enables you to see where you're headed over the medium to long term, but once you have your longer-term forecast you'll want to shorten this up. Being clear on where you expect to be a year from now is an important step in this process.

Having solid long-term goals is important, but breaking these long-term goals down into shorter-term targets is powerful. It makes your money work more tangible, which in turn makes your big goals more achievable.

Once you have your one-year goal, you can break that down into smaller, monthly targets. Again, this makes the work you need to do right now seem much more manageable.

Table 9.1 shows the tracker we use for this. You can make your own or download our template at https://bit.ly/virginmillionaire.

Table 9.1 calculating your net wealth position

	Current ($)	+1 month ($)	+12 months ($)
Working cash	6350	6350	6350
Long-term savings	15000	15500	21500
Share investments	5000	5500	11900
Property investments	725000	727917	761250
Investment debt	550000	550000	550000
Own home	–	–	–
Home mortgage	–	–	–
Superannuation 1	156000	156900	166000
Superannuation 2	–	–	–
Total net wealth	**$357350**	**$362167**	**$417000**

You now have your bigger goals and a crystal-clear path to get there, knowing exactly what you need to do in the next 30 days to keep things on track.

Having put in the work, you have a solid financial plan in place, and you should congratulate yourself on getting to this point. But here's the thing: life will rarely play out in exactly the way you've planned.

Without getting too philosophical here, this is the beauty of human existence, because if life was like a spreadsheet it probably wouldn't be nearly as interesting (regardless of how awesome your spreadsheet is).

Things change over time. This is completely natural and to be expected. There will be changes in what's going on with your money, such as your income, expenses, how your investments perform or interest rates on mortgages. You'll also see changes in what's going on in the world, around investment markets, property markets, inflation, unemployment and so on. Finally, you can expect changes over time in what you yourself want, what's important to you, where you want to live or work, what you want for yourself and your family.

Changes in these three areas will mean the actual results you get from your money are going to deviate from your plan. It's important when these changes come up, first, that you're fully aware of and acknowledge them, and, second, that you understand what's driving the changes so you can assess whether you need to change anything.

Over the years I've developed a system for checking in on my own money. We use the same approach at Pivot Wealth with our clients. On a monthly basis, we suggest a (quick) structured check-in on your money; we refer to it as your Smart Money Review. I'll unpack the format for the Smart Money Review soon.

Celebrating your progress

It's in the nature of people to be forward focused. You think about all the things you want to happen and where you want to take things with your life and your money, and you think about how much more awesome things will be when you get there.

There's nothing wrong with this. In fact, thinking ahead helps drive your motivation to keep moving forward. But if you only focus forward you can run into trouble.

It's easy to fall into the trap of getting yourself worked up by the fact you don't yet have your dream home, that your savings balance isn't where you want it to be, that you have more debt than you want or that your investment income isn't at the level you want it to be.

When you fall into this thinking trap, it can seem like everything you really want is so far away that it'll take forever to get there. But when you look back at the progress you've made, some magic is created.

You'll often be surprised by just how far you've come and how much progress you've made. Focus on this progress, and the wins along the way, and you'll see and feel that the work you're putting in is creating the results that put you on track for your future goals and targets.

Focus forward, but measure backwards.

This will keep your motivation levels high as you follow the Virgin Millionaire pathway to the results you really want.

Smart Money Stages: how to plan

While the benefits of planning and the objectives of your plan are fairly consistent, the right approach to your planning depends on where you're at in your progression through the Smart Money Stages.

That said, there are some universal principles that you can (and should) apply around how and when you plan with your money. Here I'll outline the Smart Money system I personally use, and the one we use with clients at Pivot Wealth.

Annual planning session

This is the centrepiece of your Smart Money system, and everything else builds around your annual plan. Through this process you'll first get clear on your current financial trajectory, highlighting where you're headed and what your money will look like in the months and years ahead if you keep following your current path. From there you'll be able to assess the impact of making changes.

You can look at variables such as changing your rate of savings, income and investments. And you can look at introducing new tactics and strategies to assess the impact of these changes on your overall trajectory. Specifically, you can consider investing more or less of your savings, introducing an investment property, or optimising your tax planning and tax strategies.

From there you'll choose the strategy and tactics you want to follow in the year ahead. This in turn allows you to set your 12-month goal, and break it down into quarterly and monthly targets. These shorter-term targets are going to be crucial in the work you do throughout the year, so you'll want to make sure they're rock solid.

The final step is to list the step-by-step action steps you need to take to turn your *ideas* into *outcomes*, then commit to when these will be done. This gives you exactly what you need to make the progress you've planned in the year ahead.

When you do your planning for the first time, you're only looking ahead. But in all future annual planning sessions you should also be looking at the progress made in the past year and picking up on the lessons learned.

Monthly Smart Money Review

Now you have your annual targets, but it would be a mistake to think they will just magically 'happen'. You've taken the time to set up an awesome strategy with attached targets you're excited about, targets that will enable you to make the progress you want towards smart money freedom.

Simply setting up this plan is likely to be a big mental relief, because you now have a clear path to follow, but if you just park your plan and give it no further thought, you'll quickly end up in the same position you were in before you put your plan in place.

Instead, check in on your progress, celebrate your wins, take on any lessons learned and refocus for the month (and months) ahead.

As mentioned, over the years I've developed a process for checking in on my own money, and we now use it with all our financial planning clients at Pivot Wealth. I call it the Smart Money Review.

The format of the Smart Money Review is as follows:

- List your money wins from the past month. Try to list as many as possible, both big and small, and make a point of celebrating your progress.
- Note what your financial position was at the start of the month (savings, investments and debt).
- What's your financial position now?
- Where did you do better than expected and where did you do worse?
- What was the reason for any variations (positive or negative)?
- Do you need to change any behaviour or actions based on these variations?
- What are your targets for the month ahead?
- Note any key actions or focus areas, then commit to a timeline on these actions.

Working through these items shouldn't be time-consuming. It should be fun. If you're in the process of changing your behaviours and habits around your money, the first few times you do this you should be prepared for results that aren't quite as rosy as you would like them to be.

This is completely normal as behaviour change takes time. The important thing is to *keep going*. You'll find that as you become more aware of your money, you'll start making smaller shifts, and before you know it what had seemed like a massive struggle will happen much more easily.

Once you get this process running smoothly, you should find it's a quick and easy way to stay on top of your money. You'll be less stressed about your finances because you're now in control. You'll also be able to identify the things that positively affect your results so you can do more of this, and the things that are slowing you down so you can reduce and eliminate them over time.

Next, I'll cover the key considerations for your planning through the Smart Money Stages. The key outcomes you're aiming for at each stage are shown in table 9.2.

Table 9.2 Smart Money Stages and planning

Success outcomes	Foundations	Focus	Optimise	Accelerate	Impact
Planning	You're clear on your financial trajectory and confidently making progress as planned.	You're not yet on track to achieve financial freedom in your desired timeframe.	You're on track to reach your financial freedom number within your desired timeframe. 9/10 satisfaction with saving and spending at current levels.	You're on track to exceed your financial freedom number within your desired timeframe.	You have achieved complete financial freedom, with ideal lifestyle spending plus surplus savings capacity.

How to plan: Foundations

At the Foundations stage, your planning should be pretty straightforward, because at this point you likely only have a savings account, an investment account, your super fund savings and maybe some debt.

At this point in your journey your focus is clear: it's on building solid habits around your savings and starting a regular share investment. This means your plan will be a simple one, with a focus on how quickly your savings and investments will grow.

That said, don't underestimate the power of being clear on your financial trajectory and setting solid short- and long-term targets. This is crucial for giving you the motivation to follow the path and making sure you're able to progress to the next stage at the soonest opportunity.

Particularly at the Foundations stage, because your savings and investment balance will likely be fairly low, it can seem like you have *so* much work to do that it's going to take forever to make any meaningful progress. So it's easy to fall into the trap of putting your money progress in the 'too hard' basket and letting bad habits creep in.

To avoid this, focus on the longer-term outcomes you'll achieve if you follow your current plan. This will motivate you to keep putting in the work. It will also alert you if your timeframes are too long, allowing you to start making adjustments now.

Also, take the time to map out how your savings and investments will build over the next week, month and year. This will help you understand how long it's going to take to advance to the next Smart Money Stage, where things will get even more exciting.

Of the tools you can use for your planning, a compound interest calculator should be your best friend at this stage. Coupled with a good spreadsheet this should be enough to get you started. If you're coming into the Foundations stage on a higher income with savings of more than $1000 a month, you might consider getting some professional help with your planning to accelerate your progress.

How to plan: Focus

At the Focus stage, your planning is starting to get more involved as you begin positioning yourself to purchase your first investment property. This purchase should be pursued with laser focus, as it's a huge step that will seriously kick-start the momentum that's going to push you through every other Smart Money Stage.

I can't overstate how important it is that you get this property purchase right. If you choose a dud property, get your purchase price or strategy wrong, or allow your timeline to drag out, over the years and decades to come it's likely to cost you hundreds of thousands of dollars — maybe even into seven-figure territory.

This is the most important investment you'll ever make, and you *have* to get it right.

There are two elements to your property purchase I want you to keep your full focus on. First, your property purchase strategy itself: the property you ultimately choose, how much you spend, how much you borrow, your deposit and how you structure your debt. This will allow you to unlock the second element, which is your timeline and targets to execute on your property purchase.

How much you're going to spend on your property is probably the biggest decision you'll make. As explained in chapter 3, this should not be driven by what you think you can afford or what sort of properties you 'like'. Rather, you should choose a price point that allows you to purchase a property that's a great investment and will make you good money over the years ahead.

Aim to get into the property market as soon as possible, so you can start using the bank's money and the power of property equity to build your investment assets and wealth. For most people this means finding a lower-valued property that will be a great investment.

That said, if you're on a strong savings trajectory, and if waiting a few months will allow you to buy a higher-valued property that will deliver more growth in the years ahead, this should be carefully considered. If you're at this stage and saving strongly (in excess of $2000 a month), you should consider investing in a good financial plan to make the most of this huge investment decision.

Once you've decided how much you plan to spend on your investment property, you can start getting tactical on your timeline and approach. Success here means knowing how much you can borrow today and how your borrowing capacity is likely to change in the short term, and being crystal clear on how much you need for a deposit to make your property purchase happen. Once you have this, you can map out your month-by-month timeline to determine exactly when you're going to get there.

A good mortgage broker is going to be crucial to your success here. I'll dive deep into mortgage broking in the next chapter to help you understand your borrowing capacity, how to structure your debt, to get the best mortgage deal and to understand exactly how much you'll need as a deposit to make your property purchase happen. Then a mortgage broker will help you actually do it.

Besides property investment, the other elements of your money shouldn't be neglected through the Focus stage. If you make this mistake, you risk undoing the good work that's been done to get you to the point you're at now.

By the end of the Focus stage, you should also be using multiple tax-saving strategies to save you at least $10k per annum in tax. There's a big opportunity here, but it's important you choose tax-saving strategies that fit with your upcoming property purchase and the other things you're doing with your money. This is where a robust financial plan is going to add a lot of value.

You're also going to be investing a significant amount of your income in shares (your minimum target is 5 per cent), so it's important you continue to choose good investments and automate your strategy as far as possible.

Given your property purchase is getting closer, your risk management should be another focus area. As soon as you introduce debt and leverage into your investment strategy, your risk levels increase. This means your focus on risk management needs to increase along with it.

Your target at the Focus stage is to set up an emergency fund with at least three months' coverage for your fixed living expenses. It can seem counterintuitive to have this money in savings while you're gunning it to build up money for your property deposit, but in my opinion this is a key to executing on your property purchase without a huge amount of stress or anxiety.

At the start of this stage your planning should be fairly simple, but as you progress and get closer to your property purchase, you'll get some serious benefits from levelling up your approach.

If you're good with spreadsheets, you can get a fair amount done yourself. But I'll note that as you get closer to making some of the bigger decisions it will be challenging to get the level of confidence you really need to execute on the ideal strategy for you. In my biased opinion, at this point you should seriously consider engaging a professional to help with your planning. The expense will pay for itself many times over when you nail this Smart Money Stage.

How to plan: Optimise

At the Optimise stage, there is a fair bit going on. Key outcomes for this stage are your second investment property purchase, building your regular share investing to 10 per cent of your household income and introducing (at least) one non-superannuation tax structure. Also aim to max out your super contributions, build an emergency buffer at six months of your living expenses, and do it all while being on track to achieve smart money freedom in your desired timeframe while scoring 9 out of 10 on your satisfaction levels with your lifestyle spending today.

These seriously chunky goals will drive you up into the Accelerate stage and towards Impact. By now you should be excited. There's still work to be done, but from here essentially you just need to follow the bouncing ball towards true money success.

At this stage there's one big risk I've seen many people fall victim to: it's called the 'good enough' risk. There are already a lot of 'good' things happening with your money. With savings growing, investments building and property compounding, you start seeing the possibilities of the future epic success you crave.

So it's easy to think that because you're doing well, you don't need to be *as* focused on keeping your money moving forward. But I can tell you for sure that the reason you got to this stage is exactly because of the disciplined focus you maintained at the previous stages. Letting that focus slip is a costly mistake.

The faster you get through the Optimise stage, the faster you can 'lock in' the work you've done to date, then your success should come more easily moving forward. *Please don't lose focus when you're so close.*

There are three key considerations at the Optimise stage: your second investment property purchase, which tax structures you use, and your plan itself and how it fits with the lifestyle you want to live.

I've already argued that your first property purchase is the most important investment you'll make in your life; the next most important is your second property.

If you choose a dud property, your equity growth can stall, sabotaging your future investing ability. If you don't spend the right amount, you can under-utilise your borrowing capacity or burn your investing capacity, which will cost you hundreds of thousands of dollars in the years ahead. This property purchase is likely to be *the* primary driver of your wealth and investments over the years ahead, therefore the biggest driver of your progress towards smart money freedom.

There's a huge opportunity here. When you get this property purchase right, you can make some magic. Choose a good property and you will add to the equity position of your first purchase, effectively doubling (or more) your rate of progress.

Getting this purchase right also means choosing the property value that perfectly balances the growth you want in your wealth position in the years ahead, while preserving the savings and investment capacity you need to hit your other money goals *and* ensure you're able to live the lifestyle you want. The right moves here will also deliver some serious tax savings today and into the future, creating more money you can use to save, invest and direct towards making the progress you want into the next Smart Money Stage.

Once again, I can't overstate how important it is to get this property purchase right.

Introducing your first non-superannuation tax structure is also a big deal, and a big decision to get right. Choosing to use a bond, a trust or a company, or some combination of these, has the potential to deliver serious tax savings today and into the future. These tax savings go straight to your bottom line, giving you more money to save and invest.

Tax structures are a little complicated, and they all have trade-offs attached. Whether it's access to your money, how long funds need to be invested to deliver maximum tax benefits or the cost of running these structures, there are many considerations here and you should only enter this space with your eyes wide open.

Any time you introduce tax structures, you need to ensure they also fit with the other things you're doing with your money today, as well as the things you have planned, looking ahead. A tax structure might deliver benefits for you today but be inconsistent with the other moves you have coming up. So it's important when going down this path that you're not thinking in absolute terms about whether a tax structure is good or not, but instead weighing up whether it *fits* with your plan moving forward.

I admitted at the start of this chapter that as a financial planner I'm biased towards planning, so you can take this with a grain of salt. But in my experience, given the importance of the moves you're making at this Smart Money Stage you *need* a good professional in your corner.

The moves you make at this stage are going to deliver so much money to your bottom line in the years to come that, even if you engaged a planner to help you push through this stage alone, you could expect a tenfold (or more) return on this investment.

How to plan: Accelerate

This Smart Money Stage is the last stop before you get to financial nirvana. Things are going to be good here, but there's another epic level you're so close to unlocking that you'll want to crack on.

The good news is that at this point your work is actually going to get a lot easier. No one gets to the Accelerate stage by accident; it's only with focus, solid planning and a consistent approach that you can even enter the Accelerate stage.

So the first important thing you should focus on at this stage is congratulating yourself on the progress you've made to get here. Being so close to true money success, it's common for people to focus on what's next and not take the time to recognise where they've come from. But keeping this progress in mind is going to make you feel a lot better about your money and will prepare your mindset for the important planning work to come at this Smart Money Stage.

There are two focus areas: maximising the investments you already have in place without taking on any more risk than you need, and planning your ideal lifestyle spending and saving plan.

For putting your existing money to work, this is important because at this stage you'll have a solid portfolio of investments that are growing, including multiple investment properties with equity building, and this along with your savings capacity and other investment income will mean you could likely borrow a lot more money and introduce even more leverage, which in turn would further accelerate the growth of your wealth.

Make sure both this money and you are fulfilling your financial potential, but do so without taking on more risk than you need.

Accelerate: property considerations

At this stage you could push further and faster by buying more and more investment property, but every dollar of debt you take on will eat into your savings capacity, and mean less of your employment and investment income is left over for spending on your lifestyle today.

Don't get me wrong. Growth and progress are good, but you have determined the amount you need to get the results you want. Once you have got to the point where your existing investments (property and shares) are on track to deliver you this result, there's a strong argument that taking on more debt is unnecessary and in fact counterproductive for your longer-term goals.

Understand, too, that while buying property is the single most effective strategy for building your investments, property isn't great for investment income. This is because a big chunk of the total benefit you get from this investment is tied up in the growth of the value of your property over time.

To put this into perspective, the average headline rental income on an investment property at the time of writing is 3.71 per cent; then you have property-related costs of around 1 per cent of its value, leaving you with an average net rental income of 2.71 per cent.

This means if you have $1 million invested in a property it will deliver you a net annual income of around $27 100. Compare this to share investments, where the average income is closer to 5 per cent, which means on $1 million invested you'd receive an annual income of $50 000, nearly double your property income. But it gets better with shares, because if you want your income to be higher, you can sell a few shares. With a property, you can't just sell a bathroom or a bedroom to unlock cash.

So while property is the winning investment for *growing* your investments, shares win when it comes to *living* from your investments. At the Accelerate stage, you're getting closer to setting up your investments to allow you to live from them, so you need to be strategic about how much property you own, and keep this in line with the other elements of your money and investments.

At some point you may consider selling down investment properties to 'release' your investment profits and reinvest this money in investments that generate more income. This has tax implications, and will likely be a significant cash injection that you'll want to invest smartly, so if you're going down this path your planning is critical to your success.

Accelerate: planning considerations

Planning is important at every stage of your money journey, but at the Accelerate stage the focus on your planning shifts towards lifestyle and spending planning rather than primarily on growing your investments.

You have two important but also seriously enjoyable goals to work towards. First is achieving 10 out of 10 on satisfaction with your spending, and second is setting up your money to exceed your smart money freedom targets within your desired timeframe.

Both of these objectives require careful consideration and a solid assessment of your timeframes around making any shifts in either your investing or your spending. To do this, consider different scenarios and assess the trade-offs in each *before* making any decisions. At this point your money will have a lot of different moving parts, so it will be challenging to do this planning to the level you need on your own.

If you haven't yet engaged a professional planner to support you, now is the time.

How to plan: Impact

At the Impact stage, you have a significant amount of money and investments behind you. And the more you have, the more benefit you'll get from ensuring every single move you make is the smartest one for you.

But the pressure is off, because you've arrived at true smart money freedom. That said, it's worth keeping in mind that the reason you've arrived at the Impact stage is because of years of consistent focus and discipline around your money and investing, so it would be a mistake to let this focus slip now.

At the Impact stage, you should maintain the behaviours, habits and focus that has helped you get here. At the same time, with so much money to work with, paying for a top-tier money dream team is easily covered by optimising your strategy and approach.

THE WRAP

Most people associate financial planning with particular challenges, opportunities or issues that need to be addressed. They imagine that firing up a financial plan should produce an immediate huge shift in what you're doing with your money. But they're wrong.

Your financial plan lays out the pathway to take you from wherever you are today to where you want to be with your money. If you want to be a Virgin Millionaire, this is the only really smart way to get there, because without a plan you're really just guessing. And given the complexity of the options and the gravity of their impact on your life in the years ahead, guessing your way through these decisions is a pretty insane thing to do.

There *will* be a return on your investment any time you put a financial plan into effect. Most likely there will be tax savings, fee savings on financial products, investment and savings uplifts—but the real return will come from making the smartest decisions so you make the *ideal* rate of progress while you live your ideal lifestyle.

I'm biased, I accept that, but I've seen the impact of planning on the journeys of thousands of my clients, and I can tell you this power is of enormous value and is something everyone should harness.

Take action

☐ Understand that planning is a skill and habit you'll build over time, and that it's important to keep reinforcing the habit.

☐ Recognise the key financial benefits of a financial plan, and how and when these will be valuable to you.

☐ Understand the non-financial benefits you can derive from the planning process, and commit to planning regularly specifically for these benefits.

☐ Take the time to understand your current financial trajectory, and how you can use this as a tool to help shape your investing decisions.

☐ Recognise the importance of targets for driving your motivation, and set clear short-term targets to aim at.

☐ Schedule your first annual planning session in your calendar to get things started.

☐ Once you've set your annual plan, set clear 12-month targets for each element of your money, and break this down further into monthly targets.

☐ Schedule your first Smart Money Review to check in on your progress and drive your money forward.

CHAPTER 10

Your money dream team

Jim and Gina were a young couple in their late thirties. When we met they had a few good things happening with their money. They were making solid incomes, had a strong savings rate and owned a lovely home in Sydney's inner Eastern Suburbs.

Jim and Gina had two young children and were just getting to the other side of the 'trough of sorrow' (the maternity leave + part-time work + daycare costs financial disruption period). They were getting set for the next stage of their money journey, and with the foundation they'd built they had a good platform to work with.

They'd been tracking along for a little while doing all the things they were always told were 'good' and 'smart' things to do with their money. They'd bought their own home early with some help from Gina's parents, and made some good money from this purchase. This was helped a lot by the growth in the Sydney property market, but also they chose their property well and avoided some of the more common home-buying mistakes.

Jim and Gina had been chipping away at their mortgage and building up some savings they wanted to use to fund a home renovation to create some more space for their growing family. They were happy with their progress and felt like they were in a pretty good place.

I met them by chance. I had started using the software sold by Jim's company, and he was allocated to our business as an account manager. Through conversations I'd had with Jim about rolling out this software, I could see he was intrigued by the work we did with our clients.

Jim told me he'd never used a financial planner before, and after a few conversations he said he'd be keen to come in with Gina for a chat to help them understand what planning could look like for them. Through our first conversation it became clear there was a lot of opportunity they weren't aware of, and we agreed to work together to unlock it. Through this work they quickly realised the power of a good money dream team.

The first thing that became clear was that Jim and Gina had been almost solely focused on owning their own home and paying down their mortgage. This in itself was positive, but they had pretty much completely ignored investing. We agreed this needed to change.

This was the first area where having the right people in their money dream team could be valuable. Jim and Gina were about to use a heap of their savings to add more value to their own home, which would have made them feel really good but would only push them further away from their investing goals and, ultimately, smart money freedom.

It was only because they now had a financial planner, who could see all the moving parts of their money and things they wanted to do moving forward, that we were able to identify the challenges they were about to create for themselves. Once this became clear, they quickly decided that getting ahead with their investing in the short term was more important to them than having an extra bathroom, a new kitchen and some extra living space.

Jim and Gina were approaching their decision around renovating in isolation, trying to assess whether it was a 'good' idea. This is a common error that's so easy to make. Instead of looking at each money move you're considering on its own, you have to look at how it fits in with the other elements of your money, your financial trajectory and your current Smart Money Stage. Only then will you be able to see if the decision you're considering is actually a good move for you.

We started chatting about different ways to invest, and the prospect of buying an investment property was raised. Jim and Gina mentioned that they'd spoken to their existing mortgage broker, who had told them they weren't able to borrow any more money.

This seemed a bit strange to me, because Jim and Gina had good incomes and their surplus savings capacity was strong. Based on this alone I felt they could comfortably afford to fund an investment property, if the bank would lend. Not being a mortgage broker myself, I defer to the experts, but I figured it was worth a second opinion. I had a chat with one of our Pivot Wealth mortgage brokers who I knew had a lot of experience and was good at finding solutions to lending challenges.

This broker was able to find a number of banks that would lend more money than Jim and Gina were looking to spend on an investment property, and they agreed that buying a property was a smart move for them. This move alone would add over seven figures in investment wealth for them over the long term, so we were all stoked with this result. But it got even better...

Jim and Gina got a bit lucky with the timing of their investment property purchase. They bought just before a solid run in Sydney property values, so they made a good chunk of money in the short term. This money gave us a lever we could then use for more investing in the future.

Two further benefits that came up as a result of going through the planning process were a savings focus and tax optimisation. On savings, we realised when we got into the numbers that even though Jim and Gina were saving at a solid rate, saving at this level wasn't quite going to get them to where they wanted to be in the timeframe they wanted. They had fallen into the trap of thinking that because their savings number was large this was 'good enough'. But given their goals and the future lifestyle they wanted, it wasn't.

We spent some time looking at the impact of saving at a range of different, higher rates, and they decided to wind back slightly on short-term spending so they could hit some of their investing targets. Without the deep insight they gained from the planning process around the real impact of their short- and long-term spending, they wouldn't even have known that something needed to change.

On tax optimisation, given their high incomes (and tax rates) we focused on optimising their after-tax investment outcomes. This work alone added tens of thousands of dollars each year to their bottom line after tax investing returns, all money that they were able to direct towards building their investments faster.

Getting back to the property purchase, Jim and Gina decided to use a property buyer's agent to find and negotiate on the property. They figured that because they were time-poor with busy jobs and a young family, if they had to go and do the research and inspect properties it would take a lot longer. In choosing the buyer's agent, we lined up conversations with three different professionals on our approved panel, and they chose the one they connected with most.

Because they were using an expert property buyer, we were able to outline the brief and key considerations for Jim and Gina, set the target price range, how much we wanted in rent, and the growth targets for the property. The buyer's agent then went property shopping. The agent found the property and they had an offer accepted within four weeks, with Jim and Gina needing to go to only one property inspection before getting the deal done.

This property buyer's agent had a deep knowledge of the Sydney property market and, more specifically, the suburbs we were looking at for the purchase. This meant that when looking at different properties they were able to quickly identify which were at fair value and which were overpriced. From there they were able to negotiate a good deal on the property without the levels of stress you get doing this as an amateur.

Using the agent took the emotion out of the purchase, allowing them to focus on finding a quality property that would make them good money. But the biggest benefit was that they were able to purchase their investment property quickly. Without the help of a professional the property purchase would likely have taken *months* longer. Given the rise in the property market almost immediately following their property purchase, moving quickly to secure their purchase made a significant contribution to their bottom-line returns.

We introduced Jim and Gina to a property lawyer to assist with the conveyancing of the property deeds and the legal side of the purchase. We had discussed the differences between a property lawyer and a conveyancer. Typically, a lawyer has more experience and formal qualifications, which can help ensure that any legal issues are dealt with effectively.

With an experienced property lawyer in their corner they had the peace of mind of knowing that all the i's were dotted and t's were crossed. Everything went a lot more smoothly than their previous property purchase, where they had used a lawyer who didn't specialise in property legals but instead did a bit of everything.

Also, in their previous property purchase communication was poor, so they didn't really know what to expect and when things needed to happen, which meant it ended up being a lot more stressful than it was the second time around.

A few months after their property settled, I caught up with Jim and Gina for a progress check-in. They told me how pumped they were with the progress they'd made in such a short amount of time. Gina admitted that she had been a bit hesitant when first engaging in the planning process.

They had been pretty focused on their money for a long time and had questioned the value of bringing in professional help, but after seeing how it all came together Gina was blown away. She was a convert. She noted how having a number of different specialists, all focused on their respective areas, but with a clear strategy to execute on, was a game changer.

Jim and Gina's initial planning made them a lot of money fairly quickly through investment growth, tax optimisation, more savings and smarter decisions around their lifestyle choices. But the pathway they created for themselves would make them so much more in the years ahead. Their plan was the thing that solidified their goals and targets and their current financial trajectory. It also defined the work that needed to be done.

Once they could see it in front of them, they were motivated to make it happen. And in the years since we did that initial plan, they've made some epic progress and increased their trajectory even further. Jim and Gina have mentioned to me a number of times since that without our chance meeting there was no way they'd be where they are today.

Your money dream team

There are some people you're going to *need* to help you on your money journey, while there are others you might *want*. Enlisting the support of the right people can help you accelerate your results and exceed the results you thought possible. On the flip side, missing key people or surrounding yourself with the wrong people will slow down progress and hold you back, causing much frustration and stress along the way.

Knowing what to expect, who to use, and how and where to find them can be challenging, particularly if you haven't done this before. Here I want to help you understand the key people you should consider including in your money dream team and what to look for in these people so you get the best results.

Mortgage broker

A mortgage broker is someone who helps you set up a mortgage, but they can do so much more. A good mortgage broker can help you understand your borrowing power *way before* you buy a property, so you can position yourself to execute on a property purchase you really want in the timeframe you choose.

Where a mortgage broker can add value

A mortgage broker can also help you figure out what deposit you need, which is particularly important when buying your first property. They can also help you understand which home buyer schemes and grants you might be eligible for and help shape your property purchase strategy and timelines.

Once you own property, a broker can help ensure you've got the best deal on your mortgage today and in the years ahead. In Australia, a bank 'loyalty tax' can be seriously costly. This tax comes about because the banks are often competing for new business customers, so they offer sweeter deals and better pricing to entice people to move their mortgage.

As an existing customer, you don't get the same love, so typically your mortgage interest rate will become less competitive over time. The short version is that if you set up a mortgage and then don't change it for a number of years, you're probably paying more than you have to. The statistics show that the difference between the interest rate offered for new vs existing customers in Australia ranges between 0.5 per cent and 1 per cent.

Virgin Millionaires understand the power and importance of leverage in a strategy and almost by definition will end up with a substantial amount of debt, particularly while you're in peak asset-building mode. Given that the average mortgage size (for one property) in Australia is over $600 000, paying even a slightly higher interest rate will be seriously costly.

Paying 0.5 per cent to 1 per cent more in interest on a $600k mortgage means paying between $3000 and $6000 more in interest *every single year*. If you want to maximise the money you have available for investing and wealth building, you need to keep your mortgage interest rates competitive.

A good broker will check in on your existing mortgages periodically, ensuring you've got the best rate. They can negotiate with your existing bank to get you a sharper deal *without* having to switch your mortgage, or they can help you switch if that's going to be more beneficial.

The other area where a mortgage broker can be a huge help once you own property is when it comes to getting set up for your *next* property purchase. A good mortgage broker will be able to see how much equity you have in your existing property and how much you're saving, then go out and find the lenders that are going to be most suitable for your next purchase. They will know which banks will give you the best outcome, and which will allow you to borrow more money sooner so you can build your investments faster. Further, a good broker will help you structure your debt in the best way to maximise your borrowing ability into the future.

It's important to note that you should only do this in conjunction with a solid financial plan where your risk is managed. Borrowing as much money as the bank will lend as soon as they will lend it can lead to trouble. But if you've got a solid plan in place and a property fits, you won't want to wait any longer than you absolutely need to.

Mortgage brokers are paid by the bank through a commission payment when they help you set up a new mortgage. This commission payment may seem like a conflict of interest for two reasons. First, you might be wondering if your mortgage would be cheaper if you went directly to the bank. And second, if your broker gets paid more when you borrow more, they could push you to borrow at a higher level.

First, the interest rate and cost of your mortgage, whether you go directly to a bank or apply through a broker, is exactly the same. In fact, it's often cheaper going through a mortgage broker because they're able to negotiate a better deal with the bank on your behalf.

On the second point — of a broker pushing you to borrow more so they get paid more — my opinion is that you need to take personal responsibility and accountability for your property purchase. Your plan is the *only* thing that should drive when and how much money you invest in property and how much you borrow. Any time you purchase a property, you should be setting a clear strategy *first* and then executing on that strategy. This means it shouldn't matter what anyone is telling you; what really matters is what the *numbers* say.

For these reasons, coupled with the fact that having the support of a good mortgage broker is entirely free, I think a good broker is a non-negotiable dream team member—and one of the first people you'll want in your corner.

What to look for in a mortgage broker

Not all mortgage brokers are made equal, so you'll want to choose yours carefully. A good broker will add a lot of value, but an average or not-so-good broker can take a serious amount away. When choosing a mortgage broker, there are a few things you should look for to position yourself to get the best results.

One of the most important things to look for is that a broker can set up mortgages with a wide range of lenders. It gets a bit technical here, but basically every mortgage broker needs to be registered with a bank before they can help their customers set up new loans with that particular bank.

If your mortgage broker is registered with only a small number of banks, it can mean the options they have available to them (and you) are limited. On the flip side, if your broker is registered with most (or all) banks, it means they can use any mortgage available in the country that might be right for you.

More is definitely more, so when choosing your mortgage broker, ask them which lenders they can use and which they can't, to get a sense of how much choice they're going to be able to offer you.

You'll also want to look for a mortgage broker who is part of a company that's big enough to be able to look after you well. This is important when you're buying property and once you have one (or more) mortgages. If your mortgage broker is a solo hero doing all the work themselves, or with a limited support team, it can impact your results.

If your broker has low or no support, it can be hard for them to stay on top of your mortgages and keep your interest rates competitive. Limited support also means they may not have the capacity to be as focused on you because they're wearing so many hats. This can become a problem when you need something done quickly—and time is of the essence every time you buy property.

Questions to ask your potential mortgage broker:

- Which lenders are and which aren't on your lending 'panel'?
- How many clients do you look after at any given time?
- What does your support team look like?
- Once I have a mortgage in place with you, how will you help me make sure it stays competitively priced into the future?

Property lawyer or conveyancer

Any time you buy property you'll need someone to take care of the legal side of things. This legal process is fairly involved and has super-strict deadlines. Property law and contracts are complicated, so it will be quite tricky (read: pretty much impossible) to even know what to look for yourself.

The deadlines and complexity often make property buying a bit stressful (sometimes very stressful), so having a rock-solid professional adviser here is important.

The first decision you need to make when choosing your property legal person is whether to use a property lawyer or a conveyancer. The difference between these two professionals can seem confusing, but basically it comes down to their formal qualifications.

To be a property lawyer, you need a law degree, which involves years of intensive study. To become a conveyancer, you need only a diploma-level qualification, which takes much less time and study.

So it's faster and easier to become a conveyancer than it is to become a lawyer, and this can give lawyers the upper hand when it comes to negotiating contract terms and timelines. Given you won't buy that many properties in your life, in my opinion when you do you should make sure you have the best people in your corner.

If you do opt for a lawyer, one thing to look out for is whether they specialise in property law or also work in other fields of law. A jack-of-all-trades lawyer who does property law, estates, contract law, criminal law or work in other areas is unlikely to have deep property experience because they're spreading their work across a number of different areas. Someone who focuses on property law all day, every day will naturally have a deeper level of experience.

This depth of experience, I think, is even more important than their qualifications. Someone who has been involved in 100 property transactions is going to have seen and learned more than someone who has been involved in only 10; and someone who has done 1000 or 10 000 has taken it to another level. The more practical experience they have, the more they will have seen, the better they'll be able to guide you to avoid mistakes, and the more likely you are to get a good result.

The final factor you should be looking for in this money dream team member is how well they communicate. As noted, timelines and deadlines around property buying and selling are critical. You need a professional who communicates clearly exactly what you need to do and when. This way the property buying process will come together as smoothly as possible.

Questions to ask your property legal person:

- Are you a conveyancer or a lawyer? What are your qualifications?
- How much experience do you have? How long have you been working with property, and how many property transactions have you been involved in?
- Do you work in other areas or only property law?
- What can I expect in terms of communication through the property-buying process?

Property buyer's agent

Buyer's agents are often overlooked when it comes to building your money dream team, but in my experience they can add a mountain of value. A buyer's agent can find a property for you to buy, then negotiate to get you the best deal.

A buyer's agent can sometimes access properties before they are advertised on the public property market. For example, if a real estate agent wants to sell a property quickly or quietly (or both), they might reach out to a buyer's agent. They know that a good buyer's agent will have a list of clients who are ready to buy property quickly, so they can get a quick sale.

When using a buyer's agent, the first step is to agree on a 'brief'. This brief will cover the areas you want to include in your search, your target price range and limits, the target rental income, and whether you're buying for growth or income or a combination. Once they have the brief, they will start searching for properties that fit, then present you with a short list.

With a buyer's agent, you can choose to be completely hands off and not physically see the properties at all, or you can go to the final inspection or multiple inspections, whichever you prefer. Typically, I suggest it's a good idea to physically see a property before you make an offer, but with the right property buyer this isn't absolutely necessary.

It's worth noting that there are a lot of different property philosophies out there, and when choosing a buyer's agent make sure their philosophy is aligned with your own. Do you agree on the types of properties and areas that will make a good investment for you?

For example, some property buyers are big believers in building a positive income property portfolio through buying regional properties; others look for undervalued areas; others may be big on buying in Sydney metro areas, while still others may target properties with development potential. It's crucial that you're comfortable with the philosophy of your property buyer, and you'll want to figure this out *before* you engage them.

If you're also using a financial planner to help with your strategy, your philosophy is likely to be something you've defined *before* you engage your property buyer. But if you're doing your planning yourself, it's important to be clear on the approach you want to take before you jump in.

When working with clients at Pivot Wealth, we advocate the philosophy I've outlined in chapter 3, targeting premium properties with strong long-term growth potential in areas with strong demand and limited supply, typically certain areas around Sydney, Melbourne and Brisbane. To help clients who are keen to follow our approach, we have a panel of different buyer's agents who follow the same philosophy when buying properties for their clients.

But sometimes our clients want to use their own people, either because they have existing relationships or because someone comes highly recommended. When this happens, we will chat with their property buyer to ensure the properties they find for our clients are going to be consistent with their overarching financial plan. In this chat we ask the agents questions to get a sense of their property philosophy.

Recently a couple of our clients have used agents who followed an approach we were comfortable with and one that we weren't. I'll unpack these experiences so you can see how this works in practice.

One of the property buyers focused on buying properties on Sydney's Northern Beaches, where the supply is super tight because new building applications are rarely approved. Another bought character properties, mainly super-trendy apartments in Sydney's inner Eastern Suburbs that are tightly held and rarely traded, where people will pay premium prices just to get into the specific building. The final agent targeted houses in semi-regional areas with strong shorter-term growth potential.

For the first two, while this philosophy wasn't fully consistent with our preferred approach, it was still broadly aligned. The properties were premium, the fundamentals (supply and demand) were solid, and importantly these were the sorts of properties that could expect strong growth not just for the next decade but for the next 50 years. This is something we think is very important for anyone looking to follow the Virgin Millionaire pathway.

With the final property buyer, we weren't comfortable with the semi-regional property approach targeting short-term returns, and it also wasn't consistent with our client's financial plan. As we explained to our client, this approach came with a number of risks, including higher rental vacancy rates, lower long-term growth potential, more administration to manage lower-value properties, more ups and downs (volatility) in property prices, and, biggest of all, the fact that this approach was suggested as a way to generate strong short-term returns.

After explaining to our client the inconsistencies between this approach and what they were looking for the property to actually do for them, they chose to use an agent with a philosophy that was more consistent with their overall investing goals.

This is the sort of screening you'll want to do *before* you engage a buyer's agent. The reality is there are lots of buyer's agents out there. If you find one whose philosophy isn't consistent with yours, it doesn't mean they're not good at what they do, but it does mean you probably need to find a different agent.

Where a buyer's agent can add value

Because a buyer's agent is finding property for you they'll save you a heap of time. This can be particularly valuable if you're time-poor and don't want to spend months of your nights and weekends chasing open inspections.

I've lost count of the number of people I've seen take many months to progress from deciding to buy a property to actually completing the purchase. When the property market is trending up, this delay can be seriously costly. Many who delayed on their property purchase had to pay more than they would have if they had moved faster.

But further than just the time and speed of your purchase, your buyer's agent will have a strong understanding of the property market you're buying in simply because of the sheer volume of properties they look at.

This deep understanding of the market puts a buyer's agent in a stronger position to get you the best deal when negotiating on a property. Because they see pricing on so many homes, they'll be able to quickly and assess fairly accurately how much it should sell for. This gives them a huge advantage over you or me, as we would really just be guessing.

Apart from knowing what a property is worth, a buyer's agent will have extensive experience negotiating on properties. This allows them to use different tactics to get you the best price. And further, when a buyer's agent is negotiating with a real estate agent on your behalf, the real estate agent will take them more seriously because they know that their buyer is serious about buying a property quickly.

And beyond all of this, using a buyer's agent goes a long way to taking the emotion out of a property purchase. Because they're focused on the numbers and the brief, they will look for properties that match it, and screen out those that don't. Once they find a property that does fit your criteria, if the negotiations start moving outside of the ranges you've set, they will move on and target the next property. This drastically reduces the risk of your getting caught up in the emotion and FOMO that can set in when buying property, and can push you away from the outcomes you want from your investment.

A buyer's agent will typically charge a fixed fee for their help with your property purchase. They're not cheap. Typical fees for a buyer's agent average around 2 per cent of the value of your property, which means on a $1 million property you'll pay them a fee of $20 000.

Part of this fee should be tax deductible, and anything that's not immediately deductible will add to the cost base of your property and therefore reduce any capital gains tax you pay in the future.

In my experience, just having a buyer's agent negotiating for you instead of doing this yourself should cover the cost of their fee, in addition to all the other benefits I've mentioned.

That said, I completely understand that this cost can be challenging to cover, particularly for your first property, when you need to save every extra dollar on entry costs or risk delaying your purchase.

So if you're prepared to put in the work yourself you can save some money. But if you're in a position where investing in the help of a quality buyer's agent *won't* delay your property purchase, in my opinion you should seriously consider it. Once you've bought your first property and are getting set for your second and any further property purchases, and if you really want to nail your Virgin Millionaire progress, then a buyer's agent is someone you want in your corner.

Commission and property buyer's agents

Commission is very common with buyer's agents and can lead to serious trouble. For example, when building new properties, a property developer will want to sell those properties as quickly as possible at the best (highest) price possible. Some property developers turn to buyer's agents to help with this.

In this case, the buyer's agent will often charge a lower fee, or no fee at all, and instead they're paid by the developer. This can lead to conflict between your interests and those of the buyer's agent.

First, the role of a quality buyer's agent is to help you buy the best property possible at the best (lowest) price possible. If your buyer's agent is being paid by the developer, who wants the highest price possible on their properties, there is a direct conflict. An unethical buyer's agent could make out like the property is worth more than it actually is so the developer gets a better price, and the agent gets a higher commission payment.

Further, because the buyer's agent will get paid only if you buy this particular property, it can mean they are motivated to tell you the property is awesome, even if they don't really believe this is true.

All this being said, I know there are a number of property buyer's agents out there who receive a commission and still give the best advice and look after their clients really well. I don't suggest that a buyer's agent who receives commission is acting unethically. I'm just alerting you that there can be a conflict of interest that leads to a worse outcome for you.

The way I see it, the role of a buyer's agent is to give you total confidence that you're buying a great property and getting a good deal, so you feel excited about executing on your property purchase asap. In my opinion, if your buyer's agent is receiving a commission, even if they manage the conflict well, you may not feel the confidence you should when buying the property.

For this reason, my view is that commission-based property buyers should be avoided. Instead, if you're going to use a buyer's agent I'd suggest you find one who works for a fixed fee only. This way you'll know your property buyer doesn't get paid any more or less based on the property they help you buy. This in turn will give you more confidence that their only motivation is to do a great job for you so you use them again for your next purchase.

Questions to ask your property buyer's agent:

- How do you charge, and how do you get paid? Do you receive any referral fees or commissions?
- What is your property philosophy and what sorts of properties do you think make a good investment?
- Which areas or suburbs do you buy in and which do you avoid?
- Approximately how many properties have you bought for clients in the past year?

Estate planning lawyer

Different from a property lawyer, an estate planning lawyer is someone who helps you set up a will, power of attorney and guardianship, basically the three documents you need to form an estate plan. I'm not going to spend a lot of time on this as it's beyond the scope of this book, but know that having a good estate plan should be an important part of your risk management strategy.

This is not super exciting; it can be pretty dry and dense, even morbid. But the good news is that once your estate plan and legal documents are set up and in place, they don't need to be revisited until something significant changes like getting married or having children.

Because these legal documents can be fairly complex and difficult for the layperson to understand, when you use someone to help you in this space you'll want to make sure they're rock solid.

Look for a lawyer who specialises in property. Lawyers commonly work across a range of different areas, doing some property work, contracts, criminal law and so on. Someone who's working in a lot of different areas will probably have a heap of knowledge, but may lack the deep experience of estate planning you need.

When putting your estate plan in place, I suggest you find someone who specialises in estate planning, who should be more across the key issues and mistakes to avoid.

Also, look for someone who will take the time to help you to understand key estate planning documents and the considerations you should be across. It can be really confusing, particularly if you're doing this for the first time, so a gentle guide will be valuable.

Questions to ask your estate planner:

- What areas of law do you work in and specialise in?
- How do you charge and what would the typical fees be for completing key estate planning documents?
- How do you build education into your estate planning process?

Tax accountant

Here I want to distinguish between an accountant who works with business owners or self-employed people, and one who works with regular employee individuals.

For business owners and self-employed people, a good accountant is absolutely critical. This person will help you stay on top of your tax obligations and on the right side of the ATO. For business owners, there are a lot of different moving parts and levers that can be used to optimise your tax position, and a good accountant will be able to add significant value.

For regular employees, unfortunately this isn't quite the case, and tax accounting can be an area that causes significant frustration and leads to a lot of missed opportunities.

I'll let you in on a secret here, or at least something that's not as common knowledge as it should be ...

The reality is that for an individual, an accountant isn't able to charge enough for you to be a profitable customer. As a result, most good accountants don't really want to work with individuals.

Now I'm not saying this is right, I'm just saying that it's how things are. The cheapest price you can find for an individual tax return in Australia is around $100. Even if you were to use a boutique accounting firm that was charging you five times as much, at $500 (which probably sounds expensive), this accountant probably wouldn't be able to afford to spend much time with you before they start losing money.

What this means is that an accountant isn't going to be your silver bullet solution to saving a stack of tax. I do still think an accountant is someone you should have in your corner, but it's important you come into this relationship with the right expectations.

Because your accountant can't afford to spend a lot of time holding your hand through the tax return process, the more knowledge you have about how to maximise your tax return, the better off you'll be. This book, and especially chapters 7 and 8, are a good starting point, and building on this knowledge over time will further improve your results.

To get the most out of a relationship with an accountant, you need to come into it with an understanding of tax deductions, what you can claim and what you can't. You should also be aware of the strategies you can use to save tax and consider how these might fit with your other money goals. And you should understand investment tax and tax structures, and the tools you can use to optimise your tax moving forward.

If you already have a financial planner in your corner, they will be the main driver of your work around tax planning and strategy. But even if you do have a financial planner, it's important to build up your own understanding and knowledge.

Know also that an accountant is looking backwards, getting you the best tax outcome for what's already happened. They're not looking ahead to how you can save the most tax moving forward, which is most likely where the biggest opportunity sits for you. Accountants also look at tax in isolation, rather than as part of your overall strategy. This means they might make tax-saving suggestions that don't fit in with the other things you're looking to do with your money.

Even if your accountant is looking forward, because they're not fully across your lifestyle and longer-term saving and spending plan, they're unlikely to be able to drive tax optimisation effectively in the way you need to get the results you want. If you want to nail your tax outcomes, you should look to use an accountant in conjunction with a rock-solid financial plan.

Questions to ask your accountant:

- Do you work on a fixed fee or an hourly rate, and how much will you charge?

- How will you help me build my knowledge about how I can save tax not only this year but in the years ahead?
- What sort of clients do you work with and what areas do you specialise in?
- How much time can I expect to spend with you going through the tax return process?
- What support do you have around you to ensure I receive a quality level of service?

Financial adviser

I hope by now you've got a solid sense of what a financial adviser does, where they might be able to help and where they should add value to what's going on with your money. There are a few things to be aware of when looking for a financial adviser.

Note that in this section I'm referring to a financial adviser who helps with all of your money issues: your overall financial plan, investment plan and tax optimisation plan — all built around the lifestyle you want to live and your saving and spending plan. Other financial advisers may focus on only one or a couple of areas, like investing in shares, insurance or superannuation. Such advisers can be helpful if you have a specific problem you're trying to solve but are going to be less helpful if you just want someone to generally help you 'nail it with your money'.

One of the most important things to look for when choosing a financial adviser is their philosophy around investing and money. You'll want to make sure their take on things is fully aligned with yours, and it's mission critical you do this *before* you start searching for your adviser. When I refer to your financial adviser's philosophy, what I mean is the approach they take around share investing (active vs passive), their approach to property investing and their overall approach to building your wealth and investments.

To make this concrete with an example, at Pivot Wealth our philosophy around share investing is to invest passively in index funds. For property we advocate buying premium properties and holding them for the long term. Our overall philosophy around money and investing is that leverage is a winning strategy but one that needs to be carefully balanced against lifestyle, with risk tightly managed. We also follow the Smart Money Stages approach, as outlined in this book, and help our clients make the right moves at the right time based on the stage they're at. Further, we believe deeply that tax optimisation of your strategy, particularly around investing, is a huge opportunity and should be a key financial focus.

If you aren't clear on your own philosophy first, it's easy to get swept up in a conversation with an adviser and get taken along for the ride. Because you don't (yet) have a deep understanding of all the considerations around money, your adviser can start talking about things that are 'a good idea', and naturally you find yourself agreeing with them. This can lead to trouble, because as you start learning more you may find their approach isn't consistent with what you think is important, so you then have to unwind things.

So take the time to do your research and set your philosophy *first*, then screen advisers against this philosophy and you'll be better positioned to get great results from the start.

When choosing an adviser you should also look at their fee model. There are two broad approaches here: fixed fee for service, and asset- or commission-based fee structures.

With a fixed fee for service, the only way your adviser will be paid is through fixed, dollar-based fees. Fewer than 1 per cent of financial advisers in Australia charge this way, so if you want to follow this approach it will mean your pool of potential advisers is going to be much smaller, but I think it's worth the extra research.

Under a fixed fee for service model you're clear on what your financial adviser will charge and exactly what they're paid *before* you choose to work with them. They won't be paid any more whether you invest in shares vs through your super vs saving in cash vs paying down debt.

Again, I admit to being a little biased towards thinking this is the best approach, because this is how we work with clients at Pivot Wealth. But I do think that when you use an adviser who charges in this way, you'll know that their only motivation is to get you epic results so you continue working with them forever.

That said, I personally know of a number of advisers who use a different fee structure and still do great work, so this isn't to say 'fixed fee' is the only way to go. But in my opinion, when your adviser is getting paid more when you invest in shares vs property or anything else, it can undermine the confidence I think you should get from your financial plan.

You should also know that cheapest isn't best when it comes to financial advice, and you get what you pay for. Creating a financial plan is in itself simple, but creating one that will actually work is harder, more involved and more time-consuming, and it will cost you more.

Ultimately, it's not a financial plan you want so much as the results that plan can produce. You want a premium solution that will actually deliver outcomes. A cheap adviser probably won't be able to deliver the level of support you need to get maximum results in the shortest possible time. Cheap advice will often cost you a lot more than the price you pay, in terms of missed opportunities, lost time and more stress along the way.

After fees and philosophy, the next most important thing to look for is that your financial adviser has deep experience in solving the problems you might be facing, taking advantage of the opportunities available to you and avoiding the common mistakes that can hold you back.

It's impossible to be all things to all people and to be an expert in everything. Some advisers specialise in working with retirees, business owners, high-net-worth individuals, young people, old people, and all shapes and sizes in between. If your adviser works with everyone, it's unlikely they're going to be an expert in any one space.

But if your adviser is working with people like you day in and day out, they will have seen more of the good, the bad and the ugly you may encounter. This puts them into a stronger position to get you the best results out of your money.

Another thing you'll want to look for is that your adviser has a good level of support around them, and that the business is large enough to ensure you get looked after not just today but into the years ahead.

Money success is a long-term game, so while you don't have to commit to working with an adviser forever from the start, this should be on your radar. If your adviser is a solo hero, a business owner trying to focus on growing and managing a business alongside looking after their clients, or someone with a huge number of clients, delivering the high level of service needed to ensure your relationship is successful long term may not be possible.

The final element you should focus on when choosing an adviser is how they'll ensure your awesome financial plan turns into awesome financial outcomes and results. I've definitely been guilty of getting excited about putting together a financial plan for someone, before reminding myself that the *plan* is only a tool that's used as a stepping stone to achieving *results*.

When you're using a financial adviser, the goal isn't the financial plan. The real goal is getting more money in your investment account, more investment income, more tax savings or whatever other financial results are important to you. So when you engage a financial planner, take the time to understand specifically how they'll help you drive these results.

There are lots of different approaches that can work to deliver results, but part of this is how you set up 'systems' around your saving, money management, investing and debt reduction.

A clear bank account structure to automate your savings and an automated way to invest and pay down debt will systemise your money management and investing. And a system around your planning and checking in on your progress that's broadly aligned with the elements covered in the previous chapter will keep everything moving forward and on track.

Questions to ask your financial adviser:

- What is your experience working with people like me?
- What sorts of results should I expect from your advice, and where will I see the value?
- How do you charge fees?
- How much of your advice involves me making decisions vs you telling me what will be best?
- How do you balance lifestyle and financial goals in your planning and advice?
- Where does education fit into your advice process?
- What do you do in the initial planning stages to ensure my plan turns into results?
- What do you do through your ongoing service to ensure I'm getting the results I've planned for?

Smart Money Stages and your money dream team

The key considerations around your money dream team will evolve as you progress through the Smart Money Stages, so I'll now outline the things for you to keep in mind at each stage.

Money dream team: Foundations

At the Foundations stage, as you're just getting started, you probably won't have many people in your money dream team, but you will start doing the work that allows you to build out your team over time.

At this stage you should focus on shaping your money and investing philosophies—that is, your approach to investing with shares, property and your money overall—so as you progress you'll be able to move quickly.

You might include a tax accountant at this point, but given your money should be super simple at this point you may also choose to manage your tax returns on your own. Either way, you should be building your tax knowledge to help with your tax saving and tax planning.

For both shaping your philosophies and building your tax knowledge, you will likely accelerate your progress by using a range of quality educational tools. This book offers a great start, but more reading and learning will help you progress to the next stage faster. Consider using an education solution such as the Pivot Smart Money Accelerator (www.pivotwealth.com.au/sma) to accelerate your knowledge building.

Property is going to be the focus for the next stage, but bonus points if you start doing your research early around mortgage brokers and property lawyers. This way you'll have a head start when it comes time to buy your first property.

At the Foundations stage you probably don't *need* a financial adviser, but if you're saving strongly it may be worth considering.

Money dream team: Focus

At this stage your big goal is to buy your first investment property. As noted in the previous chapter, this is one of the most important moves you'll *ever* make with your money.

A good mortgage broker is mission critical here, and the right financial adviser is likely to give you a big return on your investment.

A property buyer's agent can be a valuable addition to your team, helping you find and buy your property sooner and getting a better deal. In my opinion, this should be seriously considered as long as funding the associated costs doesn't cause a big delay in your property purchase.

You'll definitely need a property lawyer or conveyancer to help with this purchase, and you should choose this person well before you start shopping for properties. With a mortgage broker in your corner, you can ask them for some suggestions to start building your short list.

Once you own the property, tax planning becomes more valuable so you'll need a tax accountant and should also consider engaging a good estate planner to make sure your wills and legals are squared away.

Money dream team: Optimise

At the Optimise stage, you've a lot more going on with your money, which means more complexity, and more areas in which these professionals will be able to add value. At this stage you're shaping up for your second property purchase, building up share investing to 10 per cent of your income and looking to introduce non-superannuation tax structures—all moves that are highly valuable when you get them right.

At this point having a good financial adviser is less optional and more necessary, because with all the things going on at this stage it will be easy for them to add value well in excess of their fee. There's also greater potential for you to miss opportunities or make mistakes without good support.

At the Optimise stage you'll have existing mortgage debt and will be looking to get more, so a mortgage broker has an important role in your dream team. Your broker should be proactively looking after your mortgages and adding clear value. (If not, you may need to look for a replacement.)

If you haven't used a buyer's agent for previous property purchases, consider introducing one at this stage. Given you're likely buying with equity and have more money behind you, the cost shouldn't be prohibitive, but the value added can be huge. A buyer's agent will make your future property purchases happen faster with less stress and less emotion, while taking less of your time and mental bandwidth.

By this point you should also have your accountant, property lawyer and estate planner in place and ready to act when needed.

Money dream team: Accelerate

By this stage the amount of money and investments you have dictates that every seat on your dream team should be filled by a quality professional who knows their business inside out. These are people who can be relied on to proactively deliver you the best results possible in their space.

One thing to keep in mind at this point, particularly if you have professionals with whom you've been working for a number of years: the thinking, actions and approach that helped you progress through the early stages of your money journey often aren't the same as those that will help you through the later stages to smart money freedom.

This may mean your current team members are not the best people to guide you through Accelerate and into Impact. This can be a sticking point, as you often build good relationships and a personal connection with these people and feel bad to move on. But never forget that smart money freedom is your ultimate goal, and you can't put this at risk just because you like someone or because they remember the name of your Cavoodle.

It may be, though, that the professionals you are already working with are just the people you need. Make sure they're equipped to help you solve the challenges ahead and maximise the opportunities both now and coming up, rather than where you were before.

Money dream team: Impact

At this point, given the amount of money and investments you'll have in place, you'll want a dream team stacked with A-grade players. Having the best in the business behind you means your money dream team will know all the tricks, tactics and strategies that can help you get ever more out of the money you have. Given the money you have behind you now, the cost of premium advice will be easily covered, with plenty of profit left over.

THE WRAP

Money can be hard. There are a lot of complexities, changing rules and trade-offs to be considered and leveraged to make the most out of the money you have. This can be a little (sometimes very) overwhelming, but the good news is that you don't need to do it all on your own.

Your money dream team is your secret weapon. It will help you progress through the Smart Money Stages faster, taking you further than you probably thought possible. The smartest Virgin Millionaires pick up on this early and apply the same focus they have on their saving and investing to building their money dream team.

The reality is that you only have so many hours in the day, so much knowledge you can apply, and so much mental bandwidth you can direct to your money. But your dream team is an amplifier that will deliver leveraged results. A small amount of time and some money will equip you with multiple brains and skill sets, and more time directed to growing your money and smashing through your targets.

Virgin Millionaires typically haven't had a lot of exposure to using financial professionals in the past, and there are common myths surrounding this space that can hold you back from getting the results you want and deserve. Many people think you don't need a money dream team *until* you get rich. Falling into this thinking trap will cost you a lot of money, and a serious amount of lost time, because in reality the opposite is true: you need to build your money dream team *to help you get rich*.

So take the time to understand where, how and when your money dream team members can add value, and bring them in at the earliest opportunity. This will crank up your momentum and help you progress through the Smart Money Stages faster and more easily.

When choosing your dream team members, use the questions proposed in this chapter as a guide to ensure you only bring in quality professionals, and as you move forward monitor their work to ensure they continue to deliver for you.

This can be a confusing space, but it doesn't need to be. Hiring and managing people in any professional context is a skill you build over time. Don't feel bad if you don't nail it from the start; recognise that this is another money skill you're building for the future. In time you'll discover that having the right money dream team around you will be an absolute game changer.

Take action

- Learn how a mortgage broker can help you with your debt and debt strategy.

- Understand the difference between a property lawyer and a conveyancer and choose the right approach for you.

- Learn how a property buyer's agent can help you get better results when you buy property.

- Recognise that an accountant isn't a silver bullet for your tax planning, but that a good one can add serious value.

- Consider when might be the right time to bring a financial adviser into your planning.

- Understand the screening questions you can use when selecting your dream team members.

- Start building your money dream team *before* you have an urgent need for these key people.

Bonus: Take action with more confidence

This book sets out a step-by-step game plan to follow to become a Virgin Millionaire, but ideas without action are worthless. To make your next steps easier, I've put together some free bonus training, where I'll personally guide you through implementing the learnings from the book so you can fast-track your results.

Scan the code below to unlock this bonus chapter of *Virgin Millionaire*:

Conclusion:
Your next steps

I'm not going to sugar-coat it. To achieve real money success and become a Virgin Millionaire, there's some serious work to be done, but the results will be worth it.

Your goal is to put yourself in a position where you have enough money in investments to allow you to live your ideal lifestyle. This means you can do all the things you want — provide for your family and loved ones and any causes that are important to you, travel where and how you want, live where you want, spend on whatever you value most, and never have to worry about whether you have enough money to cover it.

Any time you're struggling, feeling frustrated or challenged, remind yourself that this is what you're working towards, and how epic it will be when you get there. This will help give you the motivation you need to push through the sticking point and keep making progress.

The real upside of the Virgin Millionaire approach is that you don't have to wait until you get to the finish line to enjoy the benefits of the work you put in. An important part of the Virgin Millionaire journey is that you actively choose how much you want to spend and the lifestyle you want to enjoy along the way.

The difference between Virgin Millionaires and everyone else is that rather than making lifestyle choices in isolation (you spend more and your progress suffers), your lifestyle choices and spending are implemented as part of a smart and deliberate financial plan.

This contrasts sharply with a popularised money movement like FI/RE (financial independence, retire early), which dictates drastic sacrifices today so you can live well tomorrow. That may get you to financial security faster, but in my opinion it comes with too heavy a price: wasted years and decades *not* living the lifestyle you really want.

In my view, drastic sacrifices just aren't necessary. There will be times when you have to push yourself, particularly when you're building your early momentum. But as you start making progress, you can leverage that progress to drive a better balance between living well today and setting up your ideal future.

At the early stages the work ahead can seem overwhelming. But understanding the Smart Money Stages, and directing your focus to the elements that will actually move the dial and get you to the next stage, will make your work easier.

So many people are held back by the notion that you need to be an expert and know it all to make progress. In reality, you don't need to know it all; you just need to know enough to take your next step. When you take that step you'll learn some things, and build your money skills and knowledge — and that knowledge and those new skills will make the steps beyond clearer, which in turn will allow you to take them sooner and with less effort and stress.

Your Virgin Millionaire roadmap

Now we've covered all the elements you need to know to drive your progress through the Virgin Millionaire journey to smart money freedom, you should have a solid sense of the opportunity before you. I'll finish with a short overview of the key lessons and issues to consider as you take your next steps.

Smart Money Stages

Virgin Millionaires quickly build their understanding of the clearly defined stages to money success. They recognise that these stages dictate the money moves that allow you to make steady progress and build maximum momentum. The most effective Virgin Millionaires maintain a laser focus on the key outcomes they need to achieve to progress to the next Smart Money Stage. They avoid the noise, hype and distractions, and focus on the outcomes that drive progress.

Leverage and debt

Virgin Millionaires understand the power of leverage and how using the bank's money to invest will accelerate your progress. The best results are achieved by those who also know that debt needs to be carefully considered, managed and planned around to ensure risk is well managed and that any debt fits with the other elements of your money and the lifestyle you want to live.

Property

Virgin Millionaires understand that property investing is a critical part of true money success. They recognise that property is the most effective way to build your investments and wealth. The most effective Virgin Millionaires understand that every single property purchase you make over the course of your investing journey is absolutely crucial to your success. They understand both the upside opportunity of getting it right, but also the potential cost of getting it wrong.

Investing

Virgin Millionaires know that investing is the key to true financial security and freedom, and recognise that investing is a skill that needs to be built and strengthened throughout your Virgin Millionaire journey. They score extra points for their deep commitment to always investing, regardless of what else is going on with your money, so you're *always* building your investing muscle.

Speculative investments

Virgin Millionaires don't get caught up in the hype that surrounds speculative investing, and limit their exposure in this space. Those who make the fastest progress understand that 'boring is profitable' and find excitement in making money and progress. They avoid the money myths and thinking traps that can lead to seeking excitement or entertainment when they invest, and instead focus on making steady, consistent progress.

Saving

Virgin Millionaires understand that saving and focusing on your budget are crucial, regardless of how much money you have or how large your income is. They also understand the importance and power of being crystal clear on the money you have to work with, how much you want and need for spending, and how much is left over for saving and investing. They recognise and respect how your savings and spending dictate your rate of financial progress, and how this is the primary driver of your overall financial and investment plan.

Tax strategies

Virgin Millionaires know that cutting your tax bill means more money is available to save, invest or cover your lifestyle spending, and that saving tax is the only real lever that can accelerate progress *without* sacrifices. They recognise the power of being smart with tax and using the rules to your advantage, and they give this important money area the focus it deserves.

Tax structures

Virgin Millionaires understand that while tax strategies are important, the much bigger opportunity for saving tax is how you invest. They quickly build knowledge and skills around investing tax and how tax structures and entities can be effectively used. They leverage smart tax structuring to reduce investment tax and increase after-tax investing returns, giving them more money they can use to save, invest or meet their lifestyle goals and targets.

Virgin Millionaires understand the complexity that surrounds tax structures, and carefully consider the impact of their tax structure moves in the short, medium and long term before they jump in.

How to plan

Virgin Millionaires are fully across the power and importance of planning with money, even (and in particular) in the early Smart Money Stages. The smartest Virgin Millionaires make a lifelong commitment to planning with their money, and use their plan as a tool to achieve better financial outcomes, ensure lifestyle spending is consistent with their stage, and use their plan to drive financial wellbeing and peace of mind alongside investment growth and the financial upside.

Your money dream team

Virgin Millionaires know they can't do it all alone, and recognise the need for a quality team of professionals to support the work you do with your money. They also know that all professionals aren't made equal, and that to get the best results you need the best talent in your corner.

Your next steps

Remember that this is a marathon, not a sprint. Fad diets sometimes drive quick short-term results, but their approach is unsustainable over the long term. When it comes to your money, avoiding the quick-fix approach is critical. Rather, your aim is to build an enjoyable, sustainable approach to your money. Create habits, systems and an approach that you can follow not just for the next month or year, but for the next decade and beyond.

At the start it will take some time to build momentum. Particularly at the early stages, it can sometimes feel like you're hardly moving forward at all. This is where most people give up, because they're expecting a quick solution.

But it's exactly this early, slow, sometimes painful momentum building that lays the foundations for the epic results that are just around the corner. The real risk is that you think to yourself that as the progress you're expecting in the next year isn't earth-shattering, it won't matter much if you take your foot off the pedal a bit.

If you fall into this trap, you allow your money momentum to start to fade, then before you know it you're back in the same position you were in at the start. *Don't let this happen to you.*

Creating real money success can be hard work, but the alternatives are harder. You can choose to give up entirely and live carefree today, forcing you to make drastic sacrifices in the future. Or, maybe even worse, you can choose to do averagely, eke out an 'okay' lifestyle today, and not make the progress you'd need to ever break out of this rut.

Both of these fates are variations of my worst nightmare, and this isn't the future I want for you.

Throughout this book I've spoken about the things you need to do to build your initial money momentum. You need to set quality targets for the long and short term, to be clear on what to do to get there, and then you need to *do it*. But recognise that there's only so much you can do at any one time, and limit your focus to the things that will have the biggest impact on your progress.

From there your job is simple: *just keep going*. You know that simple doesn't mean easy, and it will take effort and focus. If you're consistently taking action with your investing, eventually you'll get to a (very) good place. Like anything long term and important, it's easy to get distracted and stray off track. Good habits take a long time to build but a very short time to break, so once you have gained money momentum, protect yourself by maintaining good habits and focus.

Motivation is crucial. This is why it's so important to stay on top of your planning, and why your planning is the cornerstone of your money habits moving forward. As you regularly plan and replan, acknowledge and celebrate your wins rather than just focusing on all the work you have left to do. This will also get you thinking about the short-term targets you need to hit to stay on track for your bigger, long-term goals, in turn pumping you up to keep following the path.

The principles of money success *are* simple. Spend less than you earn, invest regularly, use leverage early and often while managing your risk, and be smart with your tax. The hard part is the *human* part, which is keeping this going regardless of all the other things that are going on in your life. That's why you need to give yourself every advantage as you follow your Virgin Millionaire journey.

My final piece of advice: *get started now*. Before you put down this book, block out some time in your calendar to move your money plans forward. Ideally it should be in the next 24 hours, or within the next week at the latest. You don't need to do anything earth-shattering in that time. It could be as simple as getting clear on your next steps from here, setting another time to talk this through with your partner or reach out to someone who might join your money dream team.

The key is to do something small, quick and easy that will move things forward. The first step is always the hardest, but once taken you immediately start building momentum, so each successive step becomes easier.

From there, simply keep going.

You've got this.

Ben

P.S. If you want some help to push things forward, you know where we live.